A Child of St Bernard's Is Known Everywhere
A Centenary History 1910-2010

THE SCHOOL SONG

1.
SING WE THE HOUSE THAT WE ALL LOVE SO DEARLY –
ST. BERNARD'S THE HOME OF OUR LIFE'S BRIGHTEST YEARS.
SING OUT ITS PRAISES, BOTH LOUDLY AND CLEARLY,
AND PRAY IT MAY FLOURISH FOR MANY LONG YEARS.

CHORUS:
LONG MAY ST. BERNARD'S REIGN,
CHEER THE DEAR HOUSE AGAIN,
OH THINK OF THE DAYS WE HAVE SPENT IN HER WALLS.
SING OUT THE SONG OF YORE,
ECHO IT O'ER AND O'ER,
'ST. BERNARD'S FOREVER' SHALL RING THROUGH HER HALLS.

2.
THERE WE HAVE ALL LIVED IN HAPPY RELATION
PERFORMING OUR TASKS AS A PLEASURE, NOT CARE.
SO LET US KEEP UP THE GREAT REPUTATION:
'A CHILD OF ST. BERNARD'S IS KNOWN EVERYWHERE.'

CHORUS:

3.
AND WHEN THE DAYS OF OUR LEARNING ARE ENDED,
MAY HAPPY ST. BERNARD'S OFT SEE US AGAIN.
MAY ALL OUR VOICES BE ONCE AGAIN BLENDED,
TO JOIN OUR SUCCESSORS IN THIS GLAD REFRAIN.

CHORUS:

A Child of St Bernard's is Known Everywhere

A Centenary History
1910-2010

Compiled and Edited by
EMMA RIX, JOSEPHINE RONAN AND MARIAN RUSTON

DESERT ISLAND BOOKS LIMITED

First published in 2009
by
DESERT ISLAND BOOKS LIMITED
7 Clarence Road, Southend-on-Sea, Essex SS1 1AN
United Kingdom
www.desertislandbooks.com

© 2009 St. Bernard's High School and Arts College
Westcliff-on-Sea, Essex, UK

British Library Cataloguing-in-Publication Data
A catalogue record for this book is available from the British Library

ISBN 978-1-905328-62-8

Printed in Great Britain by the MPG Books Group, Bodmin and King's Lynn

Contents

Foreword

A century is a great achievement and a true reason for celebration. I write this not just as a governor but as an old girl of the school; one who is immensely proud of both her time at the school and contact since.

My first memories of St. Bernard's are when I went for my interview with Madame Mildred and I immediately sensed the warmth and love within these walls. The nuns have long since left but the atmosphere still remains; a place where a student is more than just a number and can develop her full potential.

A couple of years ago, several of my contemporaries met in London for a reunion lunch; many of whom I have kept in contact with over the years, but equally there were some that I had not seen for many decades. This was no barrier to a wonderful day. It was as if the years had faded away and we were back at St. Bernard's sharing our news and experiences but, on this occasion, a lifetime's news, not just an evening or weekend. We had taken many different paths but the grounding which St. Bernard's provided has given us all a great foundation for life.

Although the old building still remains, the contents have changed beyond recognition and fantastic new facilities have been provided to accommodate the 21st century curriculum. There will be further advancements and changes, but what I pray will never change is the ethos and warmth that has always been so important to the school which I felt so many decades ago and still remains today."

PAT BLIGHT (née O'MALLEY)
Chair of Governors
June 2009

Acknowledgements and Disclaimers

In compiling this book, the editorial team has had to edit many stories. Whenever we have shortened them we have tried to keep their essence. We apologise in advance for any omissions and mistakes.

We have tried to identify the copyright holders of photographs that appear in this book. Where this has not been possible, we will try to correct the omission in any subsequent editions.

The editors would like to thank the following people for their support during the compilation of this book:

Helen Bennett
Sandy Campbell
David Clarke
Ken Crowe (Southend Museum)
Fr. Stewart Foster (Brentwood Diocesan Archive)
Sr. Mary Lucy and the Bernardine Community
Clive Leatherdale (Desert Island Books)
Helen Pestana
Mark Ruston
Rob Watson
St. Bernard's History Club
The Evening Echo

Additional photographs, courtesy of Giles Keyte and L.A. Woodward.

A special thank-you to all students and staff, past and present, who have contributed to this book.

Dedication

This book is dedicated to the memory of Bill Sanders, who was a faithful servant of the school from 1988 to 2006. His research on the history of St. Bernard's has given us an invaluable insight into the early years of the school.

Chapter 1

The Origins of
St. Bernard's

HISTORICAL CONTEXT

1910   Death of King Edward VII

1911   Coronation of King George V

1912   The *Titanic* sinks

1913   4th June: Suffragette Emily Davison runs out in front
        of the King's horse on Derby Day

1914   Archduke Franz Ferdinand assassinated and the First
        World War begins

1915   German Zeppelins bomb Southend

1916   Britain introduces Daylight Saving Time
        (British Summer Time)

1917   First major bombing raid on London
        (killing 162 people and injuring 432)

1918   February: women in certain categories given the vote
        First World War ends at 11am on 11th November

1919   Treaty of Versailles is signed

~ 1910-1919 ~

The Origins of St. Bernard's

On 2nd June 1875 the sisters of Notre Dame, a German order, purchased the 'Hotel Mitre' in Milton Road, Westcliff for £1,000. They renamed it 'St. Mary's Convent' and it was to be a convent, an orphanage, and a school called 'St. Anne's'. Students were taught 'elocution, mathematics, dancing and calisthenics and singing as well as scripture and religious knowledge, music, needlework, languages, drawing and painting'.

By February 1909, however, this early school was in trouble and Sister Mary Cecilia wrote to the Reverend Mother in Germany, complaining that the population of Southend "had reached 60,000 and the Catholics demand a proper day and boarding school for their children".

By 11th October, matters were coming to a head, and the community wrote to the Archbishop of Westminster stating that St. Mary's was "… in such distressed circumstances that we find it impossible to continue …"

The letter went on to say that, "… it has been intimated to us that one or other community of religious teachers desire to acquire this property and owing to its beautiful location this seems quite credible … for the Generalate of the Order it would be a source of great consolation were (the Convent) to pass into the hands of other religious orders."

On 18th December 1909, a letter from the Reverend Mother General S.S. of Notre Dame confirmed that, "… We are no longer able to continue our houses of Southend and Woolwich for want of teachers. Our Sisters fail to find the necessary increase of members in England and the Generalate of the Order is not able to grant or secure members from Germany. In Southend our Sisters have a home for Poor Law Children, a High Class Day and Boarding School for young ladies. The house was thoroughly repaired some years ago, the site is beautiful not far from the mouth of the Thames into the sea, and behind the house there is a large garden and meadow. Southend is a place rapidly developing and there is a good prospect for a first class educational establishment."

It is on 5th May 1910 that St. Bernard's is first connected to the school. The Sisters of Notre Dame wrote to St. Bernard's Slough:

Dear Reverend Mother,

It is not very long [since] we have been informed that you would be well inclined to take our property St. Mary's Convent, Milton Road, Westcliff-on-Sea, for the purpose of a young girl's Catholic school or college there …

… Will you kindly inform us, dear Rev. Mother, of your opinion in the fact, and make us acquainted with your own special wishes and conditions. I should be most thankful to you if you would favour us very soon with your answer on the subject.

Recommending our religious community to your prayers,

Yours devoutly

Mary Bruno

Sup. Gen. of the School-sisters of Notre Dame

There followed a lot of communication throughout the summer. Then, in August 1910, it was decided 'By order of the Superior General', [that] the school Sisters of Notre Dame of St. Mary's Convent, Westcliff, [should] cease to exist as a Community. They were transferred to various houses of their order in England and on the Continent, their work here to be continued by the Bernardine Sisters from Slough.

The Bernardine Sisters arrived on 4th September 1910 to take over the school, with Dame Lucie Destailleurs Superior, Dame St. Maurice, Dame Philomène, Dame St. Bruno, Dame St. Georges, Sister Clotilde, Sister Augustine, Sister Aurélie and Sister St. Vincent.

There were 31 orphans in residence and the school opened on 29th September 1910 with 120 day girls and five lay teachers to support the community. It was soon obvious that, for the school to thrive, the orphanage would have to be separated from the school.

On 27th May 1911, the orphans were rehoused in other Catholic orphanages. It was not an easy decision but it seemed to be in the best interests of the school.

Although the school was now run by the Bernardine Sisters, it was not until July 1911 that the name was officially changed from

'St. Mary's Convent and St. Anne's High School', to 'St. Bernard's Convent and High School for Young Ladies and Little Boys'.

In 1912, Sister Marie Mildred arrived at St. Bernard's; she originally intended to stay only a fortnight. In fact she remained for the next 65 years until her death on 6th August 1977.

The Cardinal wanted St. Bernard's to develop as a 'First Class' boarding school, but space was insufficient, so plans were drawn up for the first extension of the school. This comprised the present-day library and the rooms above it. The first stone of the new building was blessed on 1st January 1914.

The old building received considerable alterations; the beginning of many building phases in its long history.

St. Bernard's at War

The Great War obviously had a huge impact on the lives of the people of Southend, and between 1914 and 1918 St. Bernard's Convent and its pupils and staff must have been affected. Unfortunately, no letters or written memories have survived from that time, but we do have some tantalising glimpses of what was happening around the school.

There is evidence that St. Bernard's was hit by an incendiary bomb; possibly during the Zeppelin raid on 10th May 1915. A bomb fell on the roof of the maid's dormitory but slid off and exploded in the street. Fortunately no one was hurt.

The first bomb had been dropped near Southend Pier by a Zeppelin, which then travelled westwards, dropping more bombs on the town. A butchers shop in Hamlet Court Road was destroyed and at least one person killed. In 1917, Gotha bombers (aeroplanes) bombed central Southend, causing massive damage and killing more than 30 people. The psychological impact of being attacked from the sky, however, must have been much worse than the physical damage caused.

Upon the outbreak of the Great War, many refugees had fled from France and 26 refugees, including members of the families of the community, were lodged in the unfinished new buildings of the school. The number of French and Belgian students had grown because of the war, and special English classes were provided to help them.

By September 1916, the number of pupils had risen to 200. The lawns were dug up in the winter and spring of 1916 to allow more vegetables to be grown, as food was very scarce and the war was not going well for the Allies. German mines made sea crossings very difficult, and bread was in short supply because little grain could be imported.

Between 1917 and 1918, St. Bernard's boarders were evacuated to St. Albans for several months. The number of day pupils had fallen greatly because of the risk of the Zeppelins.

DAILY
TELEGRAPH

Tuesday, May 11.

ZEPPELIN

RAID

ON SOUTHEND

100 BOMBS THROWN

The raid on Southend, as reported by the *Daily Telegraph*, in which St. Bernard's was hit

The school, whilst still St. Mary's Convent in 1910.
Notice the high wall which surrounded the original school

A rear view of the school showing the original building before all the later additions.
It has an almost rural aspect

The school in 1916, now known as St. Bernard's Convent and High School for Young Ladies and Little Boys. Notice that the old higher wall has been reduced and decorative railings have been added

The chapel, which remains very much the same today, although the ornate altar has been replaced by a simple wooden one

An art room of the period with just nine tables set out for a still life class

A classroom of the same period, situated in what we believe to be the present day staff room. Notice the elevated teacher's chair and desk

The *Daily Mirror*'s report, probably of the Zeppelin attack in 1917 which caused massive damage in Southend, killing more than thirty people

Chapter 2

St. Bernard's during the 'Roaring Twenties'

1920	'Unknown Soldier' is buried at Westminster Abbey
1921	Southern Ireland is granted Dominion status
1922	Insulin is first experimented on a human patient
1923	8th November: Beer Hall Putsch. In Munich, Adolf Hitler leads the Nazis in an unsuccessful attempt to overthrow the German Government
1924	First Winter Olympic Games
1925	Scottish inventor John Baird gives first public demonstration of a working television system
1926	3rd May: The General Strike begins in support of a coal strike led by the miners
1927	B.B.C. founded. At that time it broadcasts only radio
1928	Women are given the vote on the same terms as men
1929	On 24th October (Black Thursday), the Stock Market on Wall Street begins its downhill drop

~ 1920-1929 ~

St. Bernard's during the 'Roaring Twenties'

On 3rd June 1921, St. Bernard's was given official recognition by the Board of Education. To qualify for direct grant status, certain conditions had to be fulfilled. One condition was that the governors had to offer scholarships. These scholarships formed 25 per cent of the annual admissions and, by August 1923, St. Bernard's was fully recognised and entered on the list of direct grant schools.

On 2nd February 1923, Reverend Mother invited the staff to tea, which included a torchlight procession and 'interesting games'. Unfortunately the records do not show what these games were.

In 1925, Sister Marie Mildred became headmistress – a position she was to hold for 37 years. In December of that year, a gramophone was used for the first time in the school during a Christmas party for the day students. The innovation was so successful that the party did not end until 6.30pm.

During the 1920s, there were further extensions to the buildings, including the new East Wing and the Milton Road cloakrooms.

This is the earliest picture that we have of the school badge.
It has been amended at least twice, but this is probably the most elaborate

ST. BERNARD'S HIGH SCHOOL,

WESTCLIFF-ON-SEA.

AWARD OF SCHOLARSHIPS.

The Scholarship entitles the holder to free tuition and to stationery, but not to printed text books or mathematical instruments.

Current school expenses, including text books, etc., but excluding the obligatory school and drill uniforms, amount on an average to £2 per annum.

CONDITIONS OF AWARD.

1.—Applicants for these Scholarships must have been, for at least two years, under instruction in a Public Elementary School, immediately before entering St. Bernard's High School.

2.—They must be recommended by the Headmistress of their School as being well-conducted, and likely to profit by the educational advantages offered.

3.—They must be not less than 10 nor more than 12 years of age on the 31st July, 1921 .

4.—They must reach a certain standard at the examinations held for the award of these Scholarships.

(N.B.—Papers will be set in Arithmetic and English, on work corresponding to the age of the candidates.)

5.—According to the Regulations of the Board of Education, pupils are required to remain at School until they are *at least* sixteen years of age, and parents of successful candidates will therefore be required to sign an agreement to that effect.

The Governors reserve the right to withdraw the Scholarship from any pupil whose conduct, progress or attendance is not satisfactory.

Candidates for the examination are requested to attend the School at 9 a.m. punctually on Saturday, Sept. 3rd.

They will enter by the School entrance.

The examination will be over at 1 p.m.

Candidates should come provided with six sheets of foolscap paper, blotting paper, pen and ruler.

This information leaflet, dating from 1921, explains the rules for those sitting the scholarship exam. It is interesting that they estimate the cost of books and maths equipment to be about £2 a year

ST. BERNARD'S GIRLS DURING THE 1920S

CATHERINE POWER (née VINE, a.k.a. 'Ena') is one of the oldest 'old' girls. She attended the school from 1919 to 1931, with two years' absence when she went to St. Helen's Primary School.

"It was 1919. I was seven and had just returned from a four year visit to a grandmother in Ireland, where I had been sent to escape the German bombs, a few of which had fallen on Southend.

"The aspect of some of the students surprised me as they looked like young ladies with their hair up and their skirts down. Perhaps the aim of the school in those days was to provide a little graceful learning to add to their expected role in life: marriage, children, domesticity.

"During the 1920s, this attitude became modified, as did the thinking of children. Wireless, cinemas, popular papers gave 'us girls' ideas. The thought of a religious vocation never entered our heads. Marriage was boring.

"Our own class teacher taught us everything – except mathematics. We studied *The Merchant of Venice* and *Macbeth*, acted the exciting scenes, and learned great swathes of long poems like *The Pied Piper of Hamelin*. There were Greek and Roman history, some conversational French, and art with real water colours. It was all great fun.

"Form II brought a new perspective. School became much more serious. There were new subjects to study: algebra and geometry added to arithmetic, Latin, botany, English history (those dreary Georges).

"There was also more formal religious instruction for the Catholics from visiting Jesuit priests and joy …. a new structured physical education programme which included hockey.

"Sixth Form followed this. There were only eight of us and our noses were pointed towards the Higher Certificate. There were only English, French, Latin and history to challenge me and that hurdle was passed satisfactorily.

"The gate to London University was opened and I walked through. Life has been good and now, aged ninety-six, I have much to be thankful for. When there were problems, helpers always appeared; especially during those school days when they were often needed.

"I owe gratitude to dedicated teachers and especially to those who provided the right atmosphere for learning, the Community of Bernardine Nuns at St. Bernard's Convent High School."

~~~~~~~~~~~

Another 'old girl' of the era was **BETTY HOLMES** (née BELCHAM). She remembers:

"Mrs Gardner who came once a month to teach deportment and how to sit with hands folded in laps.

"Many students, in particular two sisters, one called Ann, who were boarders. Their father used to arrive by taxi and during his visit hid fruit and sweets for them in the garden. Later they crept out of school to retrieve their treats.

"Taking flowers into school on the Feast Days of the respective nuns. However, due to the popularity of Madame Pat, who always received many more flowers than anyone else, this practice was stopped.

"Being taught sports, including netball and gym, by Miss Gibson and Miss Barton.

"The science room being opened – they were taught by Miss Ryan."

~~~~~~~~~~~

MARJORIE CURTOIS (née FENTON), who was awarded a scholarship from Hamlet Court Road School, attended St. Bernard's in the 1920s and was taught Latin by Madame Mildred.

When Marjorie was a teenager she had beautiful long golden hair. However, she opted for a fashionable short haircut. As a result, she was asked to stand up in class by Madame Mildred who said: 'You have cut off God's gift. Sit down.'

A favourite amongst many of the students was Madame Patrice, known as Madame Pat. She was kind and practical and loved all the girls. She was also blessed with a great sense of humour.

~~~~~~~~~~~

JEAN FAIRBANK remembers her time at St. Bernard's. She attended the school between 1929 and 1933.

"Being the youngest of six children, I was quite ready to start school before I was five in September 1929.

"My first teacher was Miss Sayers in Preparatory, and I thoroughly enjoyed my time with her. I cannot remember learning to read, although I can visualise, very clearly, the Beacon Books we had. I won a prize for drawing and music, though I think all the preparatory class had prizes for something.

"After two years in Preparatory, I moved into Form I with Miss Negus, and our horizons were inevitably widened, with history, geography and nature study, as well as the arithmetic, tables, spelling and writing etc. Life began to be earnest.

"In the following Easter holiday, Joan, Marjorie and I became boarders when our parents moved away from Westcliff. People were very kind to me, and I did have two big sisters, although I am not sure they were pleased when it came to darning my socks. Mending came every Saturday morning, and letter-writing on Sundays.

"Walks were a big feature of Saturday and Sunday afternoons and were very varied – the sea front, the Cliff Gardens, the Pier, as well as through the residential areas of Westcliff.

"One highlight of the summer was the picnic to Hadleigh Castle. The senior boarders, shepherded by the indomitable Madame Patrice, walked all the way – along the front and past the cockle sheds at Leigh. The juniors had transport as far as Hadleigh village, and then walked the rest of the way down to the castle. We all enjoyed our picnic and games, returning to the school tired but happy.

"Who were the nuns who acted *in loco parentis* to the boarders? Madame Mildred, of revered memory, was the headmistress at the time. Madame Beatrice looked after the physical well-being of all of us. Madame Patrice, whom I knew long before I went into her form, used to take recreation time for the junior boarders. I well remember, on summer evenings, a game that we loved, called Red Light. It was a mixture of 'Grandmother's Footsteps' and hard running round the playground.

"Madame Isobel was responsible for organising the needlework of the school and each summer there was a magnificent exhibition of all kinds of needlework, including most beautiful embroidery, as well as dressmaking and plain needlework.

"Looking back, life out of school seemed to figure more prominently than life in class. We were, in effect, an extended family, and have much for which to thank the Bernardine nuns of St. Bernard's Convent, Westcliff-on-Sea."

These photographs were used for the school prospectus for the 1920s.
Below is the playground, and on the following page a dormitory and the school field

THE PLAYGROUND.

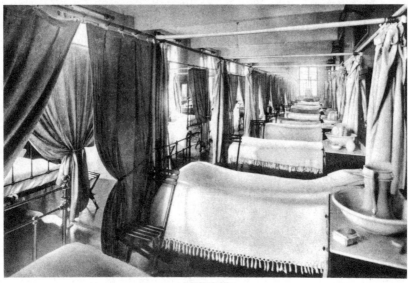

A DORMITORY.

A dormitory from the period. The accommodation is very basic. Pipes and hot water did not appear until the 1930s, and the girls have little privacy

The playground, looking across to St. Helen's. This area now contains a multi-purpose sports hall, playgrounds, tennis courts and most recently a sixth form study centre

Addendum to 'A Child of St Bernard's is Known Everywhere'

Please accept our apologies for omitting to include the following memories:

A selection of memories by **Betty M. Campbell** (née Coakes) who attended the school 1928-1937

"I started school in Madame Patrice's class- a jolly, stout Irish lady I seem to remember. I also recall Miss Warner who taught French. She laid the foundation of my liking and ability for the language- very particular on pronunciation. I still have a good accent and can read, write and get by in conversation- which gets better when I am in France! As Mayor of Attleborough I signed our Twinning Charter in 1996 with the town of Nueil les Aubiers.

My favourite subject was Geography with Miss Ingoldsby. I chose this as my main course when I went to Brentwood Teacher Training College in 1967.

A few other teachers I remember are Miss Barton who taught P.E and Games, Miss Walters who was the Art teacher, Miss Coe who taught English and of course, the incomparable Madame Mildred, Madame Dorothy, Madame Francis and Reverend Mother. If we should meet the latter around school we had to curtsey.

I remember lots of Saints Days and Reverend Mother's Feast Day, school dinners (particularly beetroot served with Shepherd's Pie). Deportment lessons- walking around the Library with a book balanced on the head, school plays- who could forget Helroise Hawkins as the witch in Humperdink's Hansel and Gretel! I sat inside the Gingerbread House and held the door.

We had an excellent education and one for which I have always been grateful."

Page 90 – Christine Robson should read **Christine Polson** – please accept our apologies for this mistake.

The Centenary Team

Chapter 3

St. Bernard's in the 1930s

Historical Context

1930	The planet Pluto discovered
1931	Spain becomes a republic
1932	Franklin D. Roosevelt elected President of the U.S.A.
1933	Hitler becomes Chancellor of Germany
1934	Stalin purges opposition in the Soviet Union
1935	The League of Nations imposes sanctions against Italy for Mussolini's invasion of Abyssinia
1936	Abdication Crisis – Edward VIII gives up the throne to marry Mrs. Simpson
1937	Neville Chamberlain becomes Prime Minister of Britain
1938	Chamberlain announces 'Peace in our time' after a meeting with Hitler in Germany
1939	3rd September: Britain declares war on Germany

~ 1930-1939 ~

St. Bernard's during the 1930s

The 1930s must have been a very difficult time for the school. The Depression was biting deeply across the country but there is little sense of this in the accounts of the time.

In January 1931, a wireless was lent to the school so that the community could listen to the funeral of Marshall Joffre (commander-in-chief of the French Army during the First World War), and in October 1932 Dr Heenan (later to become Cardinal) visited the school each week to give philosophy lectures to the staff, community and senior pupils.

Of some significance is the fact that in July 1935 the Old Girls' Association was founded, with Audrey Rose Chadney as its first President. S.B.O.G.A. has continued to thrive and many articles and information for this book have been provided by current S.B.O.G.A. members.

In September 1935, a major innovation, which must have brought great rejoicing among students, was the provision of hot water for the boarders.

In January 1936, George V died. St. Bernard's girls wore black ties as part of the national mourning. In February 1936, Dame Marie Mildred introduced the new badge and motto to the school.

The revised school badge, introduced in February 1936, bearing the three swords enclosed in a diamond shape, which still forms the school badge today

The historic roots of this badge are as follows: the founders of the Bernardine D'Esquermes, a small branch of the Cistercian Order, were three Cistercian nuns who were expelled with their communities from their monasteries in Flanders during the French Revolution. In 1799, they moved to Esquermes: hence the title 'Bernardines D'Esquermes'. The family crest of one of them, the family of Le Couvreur, consisted of three silver swords with gold hilts on an azure field surmounted by a coronet, and surrounded by a branch of olive and of rose. The motto of the Le Couvreur family was *Dieu est mon abri* – God is my shelter. This motto still remains.

In September 1939, when war broke out, the school was evacuated to Rettendon, further north in Essex, and when a schools inspector visited, he commented that they were the first school which he found to be actually working.

St. Bernard's had, by now, built up a reputation as a centre of excellence for art. The following is an account from the school magazine from 1938. It was reported that, at the senior and junior prize days, the Bishop of Brentwood had:

'Congratulated the school; particularly on its results in the branches of music, art and diction. He expressed his very great interest in the welfare of St. Bernard's and commented on the progress which was shown by the increasing demand for places in the school and the need to extend the school buildings.'

It also reported:

'On 22nd October, it was announced that St. Bernard's Convent High School, Westcliff on Sea, had again been awarded the Grundy Challenge Shield by the Royal Drawing Society.

This shield was presented in 1910 by Sir Cuthbert Cartwright Grundy, R.C.A., R.I., R.W.A., and is awarded yearly to the school which obtains the best results in Art in the Examination and Exhibition of the Society.

St. Bernard's has now created a record in the history of competition for the Shield by obtaining it for the fourth time. Previous awards were in 1933, 1934 and 1936.'

The chapel in 1937. The altar is very ornate compared to today and the priest would obviously be facing away from the congregation during services

MEMORIES OF THE 1930S

DAPHNE WILKINSON remembers the journey to and from school each day in the 1930s:

"Living in Benfleet, I travelled by train to Westcliff together with friends from Benfleet and Langdon Hills. The fare was 3d, half the old sixpence, day-return to Southend and Westcliff. At first we had one stop at the old-Leigh station and we watched with interest the building of the new Leigh and Chalkwell stations.

"On our return journey, the earliest train for us left Westcliff soon after 4pm and terminated at Upminster. We hurried down Canewdon Road, cut across the grounds of the Queen's Hotel and ran into the station. As we crossed the footbridge to the 'up' platform, the train was often coming in. Whoever reached the platform first took a long time to fiddle with the door handle and open the carriage door, giving the others time to dash breathlessly down the steps and onto the train – this to the accompaniment of the porter shouting our destination."

~~~~~~~~~~~

ETHEL SAYWOOD (née HOLT) attended St. Bernard's 1931-36:

"Rose Massey and I were great chums. We both had a great pash on Miss Mulvany, maths mistress. Just before Speech Day in 1934, we heard she was leaving and going to Chester. What a shock and floods of tears of course.

"We debated … could we send flowers? Where from and how? This took time, and the big school gates were padlocked. I remember that on our way to assembly I had seen an empty room on the ground floor. So we entered, undid the window lock and climbed out. We bent low in front of several windows and escaped through the bushes to the private gate to the nuns' house. We hastened to Cascade Florists, who were very helpful, and we chose red roses, but did not put our names on the card. Mission accomplished, so into the teashop for a cup of tea. Enjoying that, we were horrified to see two teachers come in for their lunch. They saw us, but kindly looked away.

"Miss Flexen, music teacher, called a general rehearsal for the school song and Jerusalem. I was in the senior choir. Miss Flexen missed us and asked Norah Hobbs where we were. Norah was the 3rd member of our threesome. 'I think they are not very well' said poor Norah. 'Go and get them up here, no practice until they are here.' So Norah rushed to us and we staggered up the field. We were in tears but the practice went well. We had been reported to Madame Dorothy and were given a lecture, but she was very kind. Miss Mulvany did thank us for the flowers."

~~~~~~~~~~

MARGARET GAMMON started St. Bernard's in 1934 and remembers her first few years with much fondness:

"I arrived at the Infants' door accompanied by my mother. I was excited and frightened at the same time. However, once among my classmates and being taken under the wing of the lovely Madame M. Monica, I soon settled and felt at home and happy.

"Soon it was *Corpus Christi* and although I was not then a Catholic, I wanted to join in with my friends who were in the procession, walking round the garden and into St. Helen's Church. Although I had my white dress on, I had no white veil and Madame M. Monica came to my aid and produced a veil for me to borrow.

"Growing up meant moving up to Form I and it was here I had Miss Gresham-Wells as my form mistress. What a wonderful teacher she was; how I wished she could have been my own personal tutor all through my school days. She made us 'stretch' our 'little brains' and reach out to discover how far we could climb the ladder of knowledge.

"My days at St. Bernard's ended abruptly in 1938 when my world fell apart – but I thank God for those precious years spent there; they gave me the greatest foundation in my life."

~~~~~~~~~~

1ST. TENNIS VI.

Back Row, Left to Right—
Vera Powell, Margaret Allen, Marjorie King.

Front Row, Left to Right—
Mona Duffy, Margaret Turner, Joan Lightburn.

JUNIOR TENNIS VI.

Back Row, Left to Right—
Joan Head, Mary Wells, Joy Coggins.

Front Row, Left to Right—
Peggy Stanier, Ann London, Joan Coghlan.

Tennis teams from the 1930s, obviously playing on grass courts.
The girls appear to be wearing school tennis dresses

MARY HILLIER (née HUMPHREY) attended St. Bernard's from September 1934 until the evacuation in early 1940:

"I took the scholarship exam for both Southend High School and St. Bernard's but, being from a Catholic family, St. Bernard's was first choice. Fee paying students had to pay 5 guineas per term. There were also boarders at that time.

"We were allowed to take packed lunches but were charged one penny for the use of a plate and glass, and we had to take turns washing up. Madame Bernard used to collect the money. One memorable occasion was when I threw some sardine sandwiches into the waste paper basket and the school cat was discovered that evening eating them, so the next day I was in trouble.

"On Monday mornings all the Catholic girls had to attend chapel to listen to a lecture by a very old priest (Father Whitfield from Southchurch), whilst the non-Catholics were able to spend that time finishing their homework – we all thought this was most unfair.

"I remember the Sisters putting cold tea leaves on the wooden staircase to pick up the dust and presumably stain the wood.

"Teachers I particularly remember:–
   Madame Mildred (Head)
   Madame Frances (religious instruction)
   Madame Isabelle (needlework)
   Miss Ingoldsby (geography)
   Miss Ingoldsby (music) – they were sisters
   Miss O'Connor (German)
   Miss Keough (English)
   Miss Hull (maths)
   Miss Duncan (P.E.)

"Once in needlework we had to take a stocking with a hole in it to be taught how to darn, but the stocking I took only had a small hole in it. Madame Isabelle got her scissors out and promptly made it much bigger.

"In conclusion I should like to say how happy I was at St. Bernard's and how sad I was when I had to leave because of the war."

~~~~~~~~~~

MARY CLARK (née RENNISON) attended St. Bernard's in 1931-38 and returned as a teacher, part time in 1952-53. She recollects:

"All grammar schools (from age eleven) were fee paying, but some places were free with entry by scholarship. My parents were overjoyed when I was awarded a double scholarship to Westcliff High School and St. Bernard's.

"I was measured for two cream blouses and a navy siege-lined tunic with loosely fitted bodice and slightly flared skirt with an inverted pleat on either side, which concealed pockets (for hankies only). Tunics had to touch the floor when we knelt; gym tunics, box pleated, were three inches shorter. Outdoor uniform comprised summer blazer, or winter greatcoat, felt navy hats in winter, and delightful Panama bonnets edged in navy ribbon in summer. Throughout the year we wore thick, long black stockings, black shoes and brown leather gloves. The school badge was on the tunics, blazers and hatbands and emblazoned was the school motto *Ona et labora* – 'prayer and work'.

"Great emphasis was placed on clear speech, good manners, consideration for others, honesty and reliability. Many girls were from privileged backgrounds. Approximately, 70 per cent of the girls were non-Catholics and 60 per cent were scholarship girls.

"Always in the background, Madame Mildred was rescuing people, offering free boarding places to those who had lost parents, or free uniform or school dinners to those in poverty."

This front cover from St Bernard's School magazine still bears the old school badge. The badge was replaced three years later. The motto *Ora et Labora* 'prayer and work' was also replaced by the present *Dieu Mon Abri* (God My Shelter)

JUNIOR SCHOOL
Form II

Form Prize	Dorothy Pullen
Religious Knowledge	Betty Bruckner
English	Patsy Walton
History	Audrey Andrews
Geography	Audrey Meddle
Arithmetic	Gwen Benson
Nature Study	Eileen McHugo
Handwork	Joan Brown
	Tonia Welton
Writing	Barbara Carney

Form Upper I

Form Prize	Pauline Burrows
Religious Knowledge	Sheila Williams
English	Betty Magee
Poetry	Diana Palmer
History	Pamela King
Geography	Jean Bearn
Arithmetic	Evelyn Waters
Nature Study	Sonia Welton
Handwork	Valerie Mead
Reading	Beryl Hart
Spelling	Maureen Reynolds
Writing	Patricia Last

Form I

Form Prize	Patricia Ball
Religious Knowledge	Patricia Coleman
English	Ann Flaxman
Poetry	Yvonne Jung
History	Patricia Magee
Geography	Ann Nolloth
Arithmetic	Caryl Bauers
Nature Study	Peggy Thomas
Handwork	Rosemary Ward
Reading	Sheelagh Magee
Spelling	Joan Doherty
Writing	Joyce Reis

Winning Camp on the Year's Work
NORMANS
Captain : Joyce Squire
Vice-Captain : Daphne Squire

A page showing a list of prize winners from 1938-39. Notice that the school was divided into 'camps' rather than 'houses' and it was the 'Normans' who won this year

Memories of **DENISE MCDERMOTT** (née McCARTHY) who started at the school in 1934:

"Little did I know when I joined St. Bernard's in 1934 that, when I completed my education in the fifth form, ahead of me was the start of World War II in 1939. I was very privileged to be accepted by the Bank of England where I spent many happy years. The fact that I had such a good education held me in good stead.

"Being absorbed into the ethos of loyalty, good manners, and happy celebratory occasions – such as Prize Day (how I hated the black stockings, white dress and gloves however) and happy Feast Days of Reverend Mother, Sports Day and a general happy atmosphere are memories to savour.

"Two generations have followed me to St. Bernard's, my daughter and her two daughters. I remain good friends with some of my contemporaries and always attended the reunions, which kept us together.

"Thank you for some wonderful years."

~~~~~~~~~~

AUDREY HINTON (née MOORE) attended St. Bernard's from 1937-1940 and has also shared her memories:

"Names such as Audrey Restorick, Marie Furst, Jean Nichol, Joan Maugham, Pat Keogh and Sheila Chesterman were magical names that we heard at morning assembly because we were 'new girls' feeling very unsure of ourselves. We were Form 4A (and secretly envied those in 4B because they were 'boarders') just like in 'Girls Crystal'. I particularly remember Pamela Dennett and later in life came to know her as Pamela Asquith when we both had young children, after which I lost sight of her – perhaps she moved away whereas I have always stayed in the town.

"Some of those in my form were Joan Sims (now Popham and my greatest friend), Connie Westwood, Maureen Drake, Gwen Bowers, Joan Read and Mary Winkless.

"I also remember mistresses such as:
    Madame Aelred (English and Latin)
    Miss Brazier (maths)

Miss Hull (science)
Miss Angel (diction)
Madame Hyacinth (needlework)
Miss Causeby (geography)

"Isn't it lovely how these things stay with you always. Of course, I could never forget the school song, all the words ever fresh in my memory. Finally I will always remember Dame Marie Mildred, such a wonderful lady and Headmistress."

~~~~~~~~~~

Audrey Hinton's friend from her school days is **AUDREY GREEN** (née RESTORICK). She writes:

"My friendship with St. Bernard's Convent High School began in 1933 when I passed the scholarship aged eleven and had the choice of either Westcliff High School or St. Bernard's. My father was a pastry cook and confectioner and times were hard, bringing up three girls and a boy, and with a mortgage to find.

"Fees were five shillings per term, five shillings for use of the tennis court, bus fare to Victoria Circus ... I walked from there to Milton Road every day, come rain or shine. My sisters were learning book-keeping and business studies, while I was studying art, needle-work, singing and deportment. When I told my father that Madame Charlier who was French had taught us the correct way to peel and eat an orange, he groaned.

"The standard of education was very high and I earned a prize for Latin and French but my father was always anxious as to how I was going to earn a living.

"I loved the atmosphere at the school, the smell of beeswax and turpentine polish made on the premises, the cooking smells perme-ating the whole school from 11 o'clock, the sounding of the Angelus each day at noon.

"I learned to make a Hungarian blouse with smocking, I embroi-dered a cushion cover, and learned to design and print my own pat-terns onto material. Art has been especially beneficial and I have always painted, exhibited and sold my work, and even now I am 86, it is still a wonderfully rewarding hobby.

"Our choir was very successful and we brought home the cup after a competition in Westminster Hall (more expense – train fare and tea at Lyons Corner House.) I later joined the Southend Bach Choir, so that interest continued.

"Each day before going home we recited the Acts of Faith, Hope, Charity and Contrition. A lot of the girls were Protestant and there were many boarders whose parents lived and worked abroad. They stayed at school during the holidays and seemed to us, to be like a family."

These two pictures of hockey and netball teams in the 1930s show the distinctive gym-slip and sash that many of the old girls remember so well. The photo is taken against the slope in what was the nuns' garden

THE   NEW   BUILDINGS

The above pictures show the completion of the new buildings in the south wing of the school. This is the area that today houses the science department

Chapter 4

St. Bernard's during the War Years

Historical Context

1940	The Battle of Britain
1941	Japanese raid on Pearl Harbor, bringing the United States into the Second World War
1942	Wannsee Conference in Germany formulates the 'Final Solution' to the Jewish problem
1943	10th December: St. Bernard's badly damaged by a bomb blast
1944	6th June: D-Day. The Allied Invasion of France at Normandy
1945	Second World War ends
1946	Eniac, the first fully electronic computer, unveiled
1947	The Royal Wedding of Princess Elizabeth and Prince Philip of Greece
1948	First post-war Olympic Games held in London
1949	Rationing of clothes ends in Britain

~ 1940-1949 ~

ST. BERNARD'S DURING THE WAR YEARS

As one would expect, many of the memories that have been compiled are to do with the terrible years of the Second World War. Even in accounts of those darkest days, however, the spirit of the students at St. Bernard's shines through.

In 1939, the school was evacuated to Rettendon, north of Wickford. Then, when invasion seemed imminent, following the evacuation of the British Expeditionary Force from Dunkirk in May 1940, everyone was moved again, this time to New Mills in Derbyshire. Their original destination, Matlock, had been filled with evacuated soldiers. Many ex-students have vivid memories of these years.

By the end of August 1941, when the aerial bombardment lessened following Germany's invasion of the Soviet Union, the students returned to Westcliff. Unfortunately, optimism was misplaced and the school suffered severe blast damage on the 10th December 1943 when a bomb fell on the houses opposite the school. At this stage there were 330 students in attendance. The boarders were dispersed to stay with families, while the community took refuge in Nazareth House in London Road, which had been evacuated. The junior pupils and their teachers were relocated to Southend High School while repairs were carried out.

There was further damage in October 1944 when a V2 Rocket exploded near to Southend pier; the school lost another eight windows.

Throughout the war, retreats were held for British servicemen at the Convent, led by Jesuit fathers. During 1945, fervent prayers were said for the women of France, who were to be allowed to vote for the first time in their country's history in the April elections of that year.

JOAN HOGG (née HEAD) was one of the evacuees sent to New Mills. She states:

"I would first of all like to say that I had a very happy time as a pupil of St. Bernard's.

"I had a hot lunch at school each day and used to give Madame Hyacinth my one shilling each morning. I made many dear friends, some of whom I still keep in touch with and we occasionally meet for a lunch together. It's usually one long laugh. I do not think I was very academic and remember that everyone was as surprised as I was when I gained my G.S.C. with a credit in biology, thanks to Miss O'Keefe. I played a lot of sport – hockey, tennis and netball, and was selected for the school teams. I enjoyed art with Miss Holford and she must have sown a seed in me because I now belong to an art club.

"Not long after the outbreak of war in 1939 our parents had the opportunity to send us with the school to Rettendon in Essex, but we were not there very long. During 1940, it became necessary for us to move to the Convent in Slough. My parents took me, and my younger brother came with us, and I remember him looking at the writing on the entrance which said: 'School for young Ladies' and commenting this is no place for Joan. We were only there for a short time because Slough was quite badly bombed. So that year we moved, with the whole School, to New Mills, near Stockport in Cheshire.

"The school we attended was across the road and had large playing fields. The local children attended in the mornings and we in the afternoons. We returned to Leigh-on-Sea in July 1940."

~~~~~~~~~~

Another evacuee, **MARGARET BRADBURY** (née CHAFFERY), remembers the day she was evacuated with St. Bernard's:

"May 4th: children and teachers were embarked on trains leaving Southend early in the morning. It was hot, we were still wearing winter uniform, and our supplies of food and drink were soon exhausted, but we sat in that train for twelve hours.

"At last we stopped at a station – no name plates in war time – and were met by W.R.V.S. ladies with milk and buns. They had received barely two hours notice of our impending arrival. So we were hawked round the town to find beds for us all. Such kindness and generosity as we received that evening have stayed with me all these years.

"Over the next week or two we were settled with families who were prepared to accept evacuees as a permanency, and we found ourselves sharing the county grammar school with the local students on a half-time basis. I don't think we were very popular with our peers, at least not initially. We were labelled 'prissy' and we 'talked posh'.

"Teachers strove to maintain normal school activities. St. Bernard's has always been strong in music and the arts. Our choir, depleted as it was because many girls had not evacuated with the school, was still good under the baton of Miss Ingoldsby. We were broadcast singing on radio and I remember our giving a Christmas concert in Ancoats, a deprived area of Manchester, just a couple of nights before it was flattened by enemy bombs."

~~~~~~~~~~

The school choir, photographed whilst being broadcast on the B.B.C.,
under the watchful eye of Miss Ingoldsby.
The choir had been evacuated, with the rest of the girls, to Derbyshire

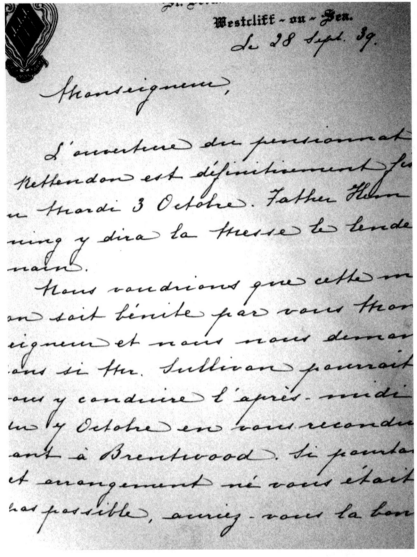

Part of a letter found in the school archives in which Madame Josephine discussed,
with the Monseigneur, the problems of evacuating the school.
They communicated in French

BARBARA MOORE (née IVORY) also recalls her time in New Mills:

"We shared the local grammar school and had some lessons there in the afternoon. There were no hockey facilities for us but we played rounders in summer and netball in winter. I was in the netball 1st team and remember going by bus to Buxton to play a match against a school there. We managed to miss the last bus back but our resourceful head girl hailed an army transport, explained our predicament and persuaded the driver to take us back to New Mills. We clambered onto the back of the vehicle, much to the amusement of the soldiers inside. We were instructed by the head girl to take off our hats and ties to avoid recognition (convent girls didn't ride on lorries with soldiers). It was good fun anyway. I wonder if our head girl remembered any of this when she became a nun?"

~~~~~~~~~~

JOAN GALLAGHER (née MAUGHAN) remembers being evacuated as an older student of eighteen:

"I was in the sixth form when war was declared. The morning of the evacuation we met at the central station, complete with name tags, lunches and small suitcases. There were many tearful farewells, especially from the mums sending their little ones into the unknown. The train was meant to go to Matlock but was diverted to New Mills near Stockport as Dunkirk survivors were going to Matlock. We were not very welcome at New Mills as they had just 'got rid' of evacuees from Manchester. We were given a bottle of milk and stood waiting to be picked.

"Margaret Rollitt and I were the last as no one wanted two eighteen-year-old girls, it seemed. But, luckily for us, we got the best billets when the English master of the local high school took pity on us at nine o'clock. We arrived at a lovely house in the country, outside New Mills. We had half-day schooling at the local high school, where I took two more exams, French and biology.

"Our teachers had to go round finding 'digs' and my sister, who was teaching, shared with Miss Negus – infant teacher. The poor nuns had a house – not very comfortable for them. Luckily the nuns were able to come back to Westcliff before too long, although the bombing was still going on.

So many families evacuated Southend that many friends never met again."

~~~~~~~~~~

SHEILA CHESTERMAN was also an evacuee:

"Soon after I joined St. Bernard's, war broke out. With my gas mask in a blue tin box, I said goodbye to my parents and set off by train with my classmates. We were to have been housed together somewhere in a large school but, due to the evacuation of Dunkirk, the school was taken over by the military and we had to travel on to New Mills.

"After enjoying some refreshments we were paraded in the town square, like cattle in a market, for the citizens of New Mills to choose which girls they fancied to share their homes. Many were reluctant to receive snooty grammar school children who were of an age to be out at work. Those of us not chosen were sent to a very old large empty house with camp beds and an enormous iron bath on legs which we called Queen Anne's bath. It was not suitable for bathing so we put some fish in there, caught in a pond. Unfortunately, when we returned later, the water had disappeared and the fish had to be rescued.

"I recall how cold it was in New Mills and always windy. Our hats regularly were lost over the viaduct, and once, when I went to the hairdressers, icicles were removed from my hair before it could be cut.

"There were happy times. I stayed with some very nice people and had one of my friends with me. Then I became a boarder and loved being part of the community. We were well fed in spite of rationing; the sung prayers in the chapel were beautiful. As part of the school choir, I spent an exciting day in Manchester singing carols in an underground air raid shelter for elderly people who slept there every night. Our concert was broadcast so that our parents at home were able to hear us.

"After being away for a year or so, Madame Mildred realised her control over the girls in the billets was limited. Schooling was only in the afternoon and in the morning some girls were getting into mischief. So we returned home, and the newspaper headlines recorded: 'Headmistress prefers bullets to billets.' The war rambled on for some more years but we at St. Bernard's were almost back to normal."

~~~~~~~~~~

MAUREEN COGHLAN remembers some contrasting times at St. Bernard's:

"In my memory, the most important and happiest event in the 1940s was surely the nativity play. In portraying the simple story of Christ's birth, it became a complete work of art, with Raphael-like tableaux and choruses of angels in pastel colours, and carols sung by the choir between and during scenes. The angels spent hours rehearsing appearing and disappearing silently.

"In contrast with that memory were those less happy that occurred during the war. In 1939 when the Second World War broke out, I was a boarder at St. Bernard's, at the age of seven. Shortly after the beginning of the war, the boarders were evacuated to Rettendon Hall in Essex. After a short time we moved up to New Mills in Derbyshire, occupying two large houses, 'The Grange' and 'Spring Bank'.

"On our return to Westcliff, there were frequent air raids at night, so we often trailed down the wooden stairs, carrying our eiderdowns to the long ground floor corridor when the sirens went off. The guns at Shoebury were a loud accompaniment to this activity.

"In December 1943, we were at recreation in the refectory after supper at approximately 7.45pm, when bombs were dropped near to St. Bernard's. There was a whistling sound, the lights flickered several times, then went out. Then the windows blew in and the wall crumbled. Instinctively, probably, or else shown there, we found ourselves under the large oak tables. Sister Mary Beatrice came in quickly and shepherded us to the front door – just a space – over rubble and through dust and fallen chairs, into a bright, moonlit night.

"We sheltered at first in the 'overhead shelter', the brick building between the playground and St. Helen's Church. The next day we scattered, either to our houses or to our sister-convent at Slough.

"There were happier times after the war, particularly on V.E. and V.J. days, when we had prolonged recreation with great rejoicing. Life at St. Bernard's consisted of mostly happy days in spite of the bad experiences of the war, kind but firm discipline and huge encouragement in faith and to achieve potential."

~~~~~~~~~~

A photograph taken following the bombing attack in 1943.
The damage to the front is clearly visible, with most of the windows blown out

Another student, **MARGARET COX**, was also at school the night the bomb dropped across the road:

"On the whole, our years at St. Bernard's were very happy ones. We travelled some half hour's journey by train twice a day. We had to be careful on late afternoons, when we had stayed behind for a piano or violin lesson, that we didn't rush on to the wrong train standing at Westcliff station.

"We did have to put in overtime when it came to the Christmas term and our beautiful, never-to-be-forgotten nativity play under the direction of Miss Angel. The play was very much the same each year and we knew it almost word for word.

"We also took part in choral verse speaking competitions and yes, our school choir broadcast in *Children's Hour*. We travelled to the Paris cinema in London and from then on the B.B.C. took over. What a day that was.

"I can't remember a lot about the time a bomb hit the school. I'd only just started in the September of 1943 and the awful event happened in the December on a Sunday evening. I have it on good authority that Madame Beatrice emerged from the kitchen area calling out: 'Don't panic, don't panic!' – shades of *Dad's Army* no less. I do recall having to go into the air-raid shelters which were on the playing field.

"I mustn't forget to mention food. I shall always remember the delicious squares of jam tart with custard poured over. Semolina was much in evidence – every Monday was it? One of my table mates was very fond of the pudding and took up position on the floor under the table to receive contributions from those of us who didn't care for it so much."

~~~~~~~~~~

Doreen Kirby (née **Bowles**) recollects the day-to-day running of the school:

"Uniforms at St. Bernard's were very strict; the school badge had to be so many inches from the rounded neckline and had to be placed in the centre of the bodice. Other rules were one pair of indoor shoes, one pair of black gym shoes, short divided gym skirt (culottes style), white short-sleeved gym blouses and navy blue knickers. Dresses had to be 'A' line, belted and regulation length. Prize-day or concerts required 'A' line belted dress with Peter Pan collar to be worn along with black stockings, however a little later the black stockings gave way to tan stockings (not nylons).

"School started officially at 9.00am; a bell was sounded at 8.50am allowing everyone to go to the cloakroom to hang up their outdoor coats and change into indoor shoes before proceeding to the main hall for assembly.

"We had an hour for lunch and the majority of pupils stayed for the school meal, which was cooked on-site in a large kitchen by the house-keeper sisters, who were always dressed completely in black. Only pupils who lived within walking distance were allowed home for lunch.

"The teaching nuns wore cream, full-length habits, with long voluminous sleeves covered back and front by a black tabard. Around the neck of the tabard was worn a high-necked, white, stiff, broad collar and their heads were covered with a long, black head-dress. The lay teachers at the school wore long black academic cloaks over their everyday clothes; on special occasions they added silk/satin covered cowls to the back of their cloaks.

"I remember that Miss Peters was a very enthusiastic gymnastics and games mistress. The gymnasium was very well equipped with climbing bars, hanging ropes from the ceiling, balancing benches and a vaulting horse. The games mainly played were netball and rounders.

"On a more sombre note, I remember coming to school one morning to see that the side/front of the Convent had been damaged by a bomb blast, which had been dropped by an enemy aircraft during a raid the night before. Fortunately, the bomb fell into a water reservoir just opposite the school, which is now a small park. I cannot remember if anyone was hurt, but I am sure that the nuns were quite badly shaken, as I believe that part of the building was their living quarters."

~~~~~~~~~~

JOAN CLARK (née HILLMAN) remembers the many air raids that took place during the war:

"I started at St. Bernard's in late 1941. Our lessons were often interrupted by the air raid siren, when we would go into a surface shelter by St. Helen's Church. To take our minds off the gunfire etc., we would volunteer to sing or entertain. I never did, but I remember a girl called Josephine singing Vera Lynn's song *Yours*. When the 'all clear' sounded we were allowed some time off. Later there was an underground shelter under the playing field. This was frightening: a long tunnel with only one exit.

"To show our patriotism, the school formed a group – G.T.C. (Girls Training Corps). We would be drilled by an army sergeant who had been billeted in houses across the road. I remember part of this training was a morning spent at Southend Hospital eyeing potatoes. We joined with the Southend G.T.C. to do a presentation at the Palace Theatre.

"One Christmas the school were to present a nativity play. In order to take part, one had to be a member of the diction class which was an added extra and cost £1 1s (a guinea) a term. I saved my pocket money for ages and eventually became a shepherd. We rehearsed endlessly. The week before the presentation, a bomb fell across the road and the school was badly damaged. It closed, so no play.

"My friend Theresa and I would go most days to help clear up the damage. We buried broken statues in the garden by the then tennis courts. For the first time we were able to see the part of the school which was the nuns' quarters. I remember being in awe of the frugal arrangement of this dormitory.

"My last year at school was the end of the war. We would watch the planes bringing back prisoners of war. My last memory was the prize giving when we sang: 'I Vow to Thee My Country' and the school song: 'Long may St. Bernard's Reign' and the school has educated my four daughters and two grandchildren."

~~~~~~~~~~

PAULINE SHOREY (née EDWARDS) started at St. Bernard's after it had returned from New Mills:

"I started at St. Bernard's when I was six. Then it was a private school and had just returned from being evacuated.

"Our air raid shelters were built under the hockey field (now built over) and, when the siren went, we filed in with our gas masks and sat on benches each side of the long tunnels. We sang counting songs like *Ten Green Bottles* and *One Man went to Mow*. We thought it great fun and didn't realise the dangers. There were three events I loved in our school year. The first was Reverend Mother's feast day when we all wore white dresses and, weather permitting, had our lunch in the orchard (now built over). For pudding we had cherries from the trees; a great treat as fruit was scarce.

"The second occasion was prize-giving when our parents came and we again wore our white dresses and all sat on the platform waiting to see if we had won a prize.

"The third occasion was the nativity play which I loved. I always wanted to be in it but was too shy to audition.

"We started our day with assembly in the hall. The nuns and teachers sat on the platform. The teachers wore their cloaks to show they had passed degrees. We said 'The Lord's Prayer' and the 'Hail Mary' and notices were read out."

~~~~~~~~~~

ANN DIXON (née FLAXMAN) remembers the shortages the school faced as a result of war:

"In 1937 I joined the school as a six-year-old and left in 1949 as a nineteen-year-old, on my way to P.E. College, having been head girl in 1948-49.

"At the time the war broke out, I lived in Thorpe Bay and travelled with my cousin by train to Southend, then walked to school carrying lunch box, books and gas mask.

"In order that we would be able to make the return journey in the daylight, the school closed earlier during the darkest days of the year.

"Wartime school-life, as well as life in general, was limited by shortages and economies. Equipment was well worn and treasured, books at a premium. No exercise book was replaced until every line had been filled, and only then after Madame Bernard's scrutiny. Clothing coupons and supply made school uniform difficult. Amazingly, everyone begged, borrowed or stole a white dress for prize day.

"Men were rarely seen on school premises. Exceptions were the Priests, Mr. Penny the choir master, and my uncle. The family firm of Flaxman's builders were responsible for maintenance and repair of the school buildings, and a cry for help from Madame Mildred prompted an immediate response. Whilst my father manned the office, my uncle Bill undertook on-site assessments."

The upper sixth in 1947-48. The girls are:
Diana Palmer, Pam Banks, Kay Hammond, Ann Flaxman, Nora Worthing, Valerie Rose and Elise Bruno.The wearing of school uniform appears to be optional in this picture of the sixth form

ROSEMARY BRETT-PITT (née COOK) has very fond memories of her schooling at St. Bernard's:

"In the summer of 1943, age nine years, I remember sitting very still with my mother, waiting to be interviewed by Madame Mildred – another little girl was already there. Our mothers began a conversation and the ice was broken. Sheila Ainsley (Coxhead) remains a friend to this day.

"I truly believe that our school was special in many ways; our education being conducted in the home of the nuns who had our well-being as their first concern. Their discipline was strict but fair.

"I remember the length of our tunics was very important. My uniform used many clothing coupons, so deep hems were a necessity. We wore white dresses on Reverend Mothers' Feast Day and prize-giving day. My dear Mum made my dress from parachute silk. It was beautiful. Everyone will remember the cherries we enjoyed, specifically picking them from the orchard. Such a treat in wartime Britain. I always remember that, whenever cherries are in season now.

"On 10th December 1943, a bomb fell on the corner of St. Vincent's and Milton Road, causing death and destruction. Our school was damaged, as was my home in Avenue Road. We did enjoy watching the houses being rebuilt after the war, from our classroom window; our maths lessons suffered accordingly (Miss Connelly was very cross). Gym with Miss Peters and Miss Western came as a welcome break. I wish I could still climb the ropes and hang upside down from the wall bars."

~~~~~~~~~~~

R. A. CAPSTICK (née JEFFERY) writes:

"I began at St. Bernard's in 1945 when the school was much smaller and I was eleven. My father had returned about three months before, after five years as a prisoner of war in Germany. I was a medium-sized girl in a uniform tunic rather large, to allow for growth. My hair was cut in a bob with a side parting and a navy blue ribbon bow.

"My first impressions were of quiet bustle, kindness, bell signals, a smell of polish and the aroma of cooking along the downstairs corridor. I was in Form I and our classroom was on the first floor, up the stone staircase and close to the old lab and its smell of H_2O. The sash windows overlooked a bomb site. We sat in double desks; Daphne Carr sat beside me and Rosalie Butler behind.

"Our teachers wore academic gowns and we stood whenever one entered or left the room. If we met Reverend Mother, who we recognised by the oval silver medallion at her neck, we curtseyed before passing her. We addressed the white-robed nuns as Madame and those in dark robes as Sister.

"I particularly enjoyed history lessons with Madame Angela who brought the past to life for us, and later Latin with Madame Aelred who was so enthusiastic. I found Madame Mildred, our head-mistress, intimidating because one eye did not move with the other. I later came to respect her kindness and wisdom.

"I did not appreciate until well after I left school how much more I had learned at St. Bernard's beyond school subjects."

~~~~~~~~~~

SHIRLEY SWAN (née COLLINS) attended St. Bernard's between 1946 and 1951, following in many of her family's footsteps:

"My mother Constance Popplewell spent her school days here, as well as her sister Joyce Popplewell. I was next in line, then my daughter Fiona Claire Swan and, due to start next September, my grand-daughter – four generations so far.

"I can remember my entrance interview with Madame Mildred and school governors. The one question I can remember was 'If you had a large bell, what must you do to make it a swimming pool?'

"One was always made to eat up one's school dinner. One day I surreptitiously threw a piece of unwanted meat from my plate into the tin meant for gristle and bones. Madame Mildred's eyes were immediately upon me and I had to retrieve the offending piece of meat from the waste tin and eat it. I was none the worse. Meat was scarce in those days.

"The photograph [next page] was taken at our Golden Wedding celebrations on the 4th October this year. All five of us were in the same form from the age of eleven. We have remained friends through the years. Sixty-two years of true friendship."

The girls as they are today:
From L-R: Angela Ling (née Hicks), June Piercy (née Carter), Olive Harvey (née Choppen), Shirley Swan (née Collins) and Jeanette Collins (née Latta)

~~~~~~~~~~

JEAN TONKING (née COLEMAN) talks about her time at the school:
"Although it was about 63 years ago, I remember my first day very clearly. It was shortly after the Second World War had finished. During the war we had been unable to attend church so I had extra instruction at St. Bernard's, and was able to make my first communion in the school chapel. My family attended and my brother realised that the nuns were actually very nice (he had made me very nervous about what they were like before I started). After the service we joined the nuns for breakfast.

"After a short while at St. Bernard's, the junior school transferred to Lindisfarne in Valkyrie Road. Once we started there, we had to walk back to Milton Road every day to have our school dinners until our own dining hall was ready. Food was still scarce and, whilst on ration, waste was frowned upon. I regularly brought home fatty meat and leftovers in my hanky because I could not eat it.

"I returned to Milton Road after the 11-plus. I have fond memories of my time there. On the Reverend Mothers' Feast Day, we all wore white dresses and walked in the gardens, went to the chapel and sang the school song in the hall."

~~~~~~~~~~

There must have been huge rejoicing in May 1945 for V.E. Day. The school was given three days holiday from the 7th May, following a Solemn High Mass with Benediction. The *Te Deum* was sung and the bells were rung for the first time since the war began.

In the same year, St. Bernard's became a multilateral school with a three-form entry and voluntary aided status. The first governors meeting, with the L.E.A. representatives, was held on the 8th December 1945.

At the end of this decade the Headmistress's Feast Day was established. The 26th April, the feast of 'Our Lady of Good Counsel' to whom the convent at Westcliff is dedicated, was the day chosen.

Chapter 5

St. Bernard's during the Rock and Roll Era

Historical Context

1950   Petrol rationing ends in Britain

1951   Churchill wins General Election, making him Prime
            Minister for the second time

1952   King George VI dies in his sleep

1953   Coronation of Queen Elizabeth II

1954   All rationing finally ends in Britain

1955   Ruth Ellis becomes the last woman to be hanged in
            Britain

1956   Hungarian Revolution against Soviet domination

1957   The Soviet Union sends first mammal into orbit
            around the Earth. The dog died

1958   Sir Edmund Hillary reaches the South Pole

1959   Fidel Castro takes power in Cuba after forcing
            President Batista into exile

~ 1950-1959 ~

St. Bernards's during the Rock and Roll Era

In April 1950, the school organised a pilgrimage to Rome for the Holy Week, and Dame M Aelred accompanied the girls to Rome.

In the same month, the school celebrated Sister Marie Mildred's Silver Jubilee as headmistress. She received a watch and a radio from the school, and trees and bushes were also planted for her in the garden. The Old Girls' Association offered to buy her a statue of Our Lady, to replace the one destroyed by the bombing during the war. The new statue was made of Portland stone, and still stands at the corner of the building between Milton and Canewdon Roads.

The statue, bought by the Old Girls' Association to replace the one that had been destroyed during the war

In 1953, Mary Bell, now known to so many of the 'old girls' as Sister Mary Stephen, entered the novitiate. She was followed by Sister Mary Lucy in 1955 and Sister Mary Edmund in 1958.

The school continued to grow and improve its facilities throughout the 1950s. Two new housecraft rooms were built, together with new geography and pottery rooms. The present kitchens and dining room were also erected, along with a sports pavilion at Bridgewater Drive in 1959. By the end of the decade, the school had enrolled 543 pupils.

In September 1955, the secretarial course opened, leading to stage one and two of the Royal Society of Arts examinations in shorthand and typing. This was the first training in St. Bernard's for the commercial world.

During the 1950s, the school's nativity play became famous locally, and it was at this time that one of St. Bernard's most famous 'old girls', Dame Helen Mirren, made her school debut. Several contributors recall being impressed, even then, with her acting ability and 'presence'.

One recalls how her father was not impressed at the schoolgirl Helen writhing in the agony of childbirth as 'Eve' at the beginning of the school play.

In 1959, the school undertook its first ski trip to Austria. Miss Haynes and Miss Johnson led the party to Fiss.

In the same year, the staff had a 'Hat Party' in the school hall.

We also have some interesting photographs of a staff v sixth form netball match in 1956, which seems to have resulted in some 'serious' injuries.

MEMORIES OF THE 1950S

One of the most fascinating contributions received was memories and excerpts of the diary of **BRENDA POWELL** (née VICARY), who attended the school from 1950-57.

"February 6th 1952: King George VI dies. I hear the news at dinnertime after gym. (I remember some of us said we did not believe it). Special prayers after dinner. We miss a history test. No homework.'

"Friday February 8th: All the school gathers in the hall at 11 o'clock to hear the proclamation of the new Queen.'

"April 1st: Our form, 2L, changed places with 2G for a joke this morning. Mrs. Grimes took it well but Mrs. Arnold and Madame Vincent were not amused.

"July 2nd: Reverend Mother's Feast Day. We wear white dresses. Our form recites at the morning concert. After dinner we watch a rounders rally.

"July 10th: Miss Hull takes us on the beach, collecting crabs, shrimps and shells etc. for the aquaria.

"(Miss Hull, of the smelly science labs, black flowing gown and the wispy, white hair escaping from its bun; she was our form mistress in the upper sixth and, I discovered by then, very kind.)

"July 18th. Rehearsals for prize day. One girl fainted.

"Prize day was always on a Saturday afternoon. We all wore a white dress, gloves and white socks. There was a concert to begin with, then speeches by the bishop and a distinguished guest. Then Madame Mildred would present the cups and prizes and each girl came down as her name was called.

"To finish, the whole school sang an uplifting song, such as *Jerusalem, I Vow to Thee My Country*, or *Non Nobis Domine*, which I remember with affection to this day."

Brenda also remembers a trip to London:

"On a Saturday in March every year, we met at school early, in uniform and, armed with sandwiches and lemonade, climbed aboard a fleet of double-decker buses, which proceeded up the Arterial Road to London. We were on our way to Wembley Stadium to watch international women's hockey. The stands were an amazing sight, blocks of different colours, all schoolgirls in their various uniforms. To some of us, the hockey was not as important as the outing itself, complete with singing all the way home."

A school trip in the 1950s, showing the school beret with badge, summer uniform and blazer. This photograph was sent in by Brenda Powell (née Vicary)

TIME TABLE

Hours.	9.10	9.45.	10.45	11.30	1.45.	2.15.	3.0.	Prep.
MON. Day I	Maths.	P.T.	French	Latin	R.I	Geography	English	Latin English
TUES. Day II	History	Diction	French	Latin	R.I.	Maths	English	Maths History French
WED. Day III	Science	Science	French	Maths	R.I	English	Music	English
THUR. Day IV	English	Latin	Maths.	French	Hockey	Science	Science	Science Latin French Maths
FRI. Day V	Latin	English	French	Gym	Maths.	History	Geog.	Geog. Eng.
SAT. Day VI	Latin	Maths	English	Music	R.I	Art	Art.	Maths.

TIME TABLE 2L. 159

This is the 2L form timetable in the school year beginning September 1951.
It shows that the school had a 6 day system, that is, Day 1, Day 2, etc. to Day 6.
Each week was different, so there was not always the same lesson on Monday
mornings, for example. This allowed for more subject periods to be fitted in

JILL TATTERSFIELD (née MANSFIELD) recalls the six-day timetable:

"We had a six-day timetable, so that it wasn't always the Monday lessons which were missed when there was a bank holiday. We sat at desks with a hole in the top-right-hand side to take an ink-well, as we still used pens with nibs.

"We called the teaching nuns 'Madame' and the others 'Sister' when we started, but they were all 'Mother' by the time we left. We had to curtsey when we met Reverend Mother and bow when we met Mother Mildred the headmistress.

"At assembly every morning, each form marched into the hall to piano music played by Mrs. Spary, and stood in a long line with the shortest girl at the front and the tallest at the back. We were rearranged each year, as we grew at different rates. The staff stood on stage and wore their university gowns (not the nuns, of course).

"Lunches were served in two sittings in the hall – we remember lovely bubbly custard and tasty cheese and potato pie – but also the horrible frog spawn (tapioca) and semolina, which usually came with lumps. Eating in the street was strictly forbidden, whether in uniform or not.

"We always enjoyed the last P.E. lesson of the term, as we played shipwrecks – all the equipment was put round the room, and feet must not touch the ground or you were out. I remember the fun we had playing table tennis with Mother Vincent – the ball always managed to get lost amongst her robes.

"The highlight of the school year was speech day at the end of the summer term. The whole school wore white dresses and gloves, and were tiered on the stage on forms, then tables, and then forms balanced on tables. Can't imagine what Health and Safety would say about it today. We all sang the school song at the end, which was very moving – I can still remember the words.

"We were the first sixth form to have a prefects' dance, and, not without a lot of pleading, we were actually allowed to invite boys. I remember our very sad last day at school, when we were all overcome with grief and went all round the school sobbing, finishing up in one of the music rooms on the first floor, vowing that we would always keep in touch with each other."

~~~~~~~~~~

PAMELA COOK (née DAW) started at the school in the 1940s and left in the early 1950s. She witnessed many national events whilst at school.

"I started school in 1943 when I was six. St. Bernard's was then a fee-paying school. By 1944, the fees were £5 18s per term, this included dinners at £1 14s; extra diction lessons, one guinea. There were thirty to a class and, at the age of seven, we studied scripture, arithmetic, reading, writing, poetry, English, spelling, history, geography, nature study, art and handwork.

"School in wartime meant there was an air-raid shelter under the playing field in the school's grounds; I can remember only two occasions when this was used. At home (I lived over a shop in Southend High Street) the constant night-time raids meant we were down in shelters for a great many nights. There were concrete blocks all along the sea-front, which was out-of-bounds. We played 'spies' a lot; big feet definitely indicated a German spy.

"With the war ending in 1945, we young ones were transferred to Lindisfarne, which was then called St. Bernard's Convent Preparatory School. In 1948, we were studying for the 11-plus, while my father took great interest in the Olympic Games in London. With no television yet, we went to see them at the local cinema on the Pathé News. Having passed the 11-plus, I returned to the high school.

"The school ran an outing to the Festival of Britain on London's South Bank in 1951; we had had lessons about this and its comparison with the Great Exhibition of 1851. Having lived through austere years all my life then, suddenly there was this wonderful atmosphere right across the country.

"The East Coast Floods came in 1953 – we first heard it on the radio news in the morning and, at school, two girls in my class from Canvey Island did not come in; their homes had been flooded and they were cut off from the mainland. This really brought home the nature of the catastrophe.

"Then, we were looking forward to the Coronation in June 1953, and my father bought a television. Edmund Hilary and Sherpa Tensing reached the summit of Mt. Everest, and the school later organised an outing to the Festival Hall in London to attend a lecture by the men themselves.

"Having passed five 'O' levels at the age of sixteen, I stayed on at school to do a secretarial course for two years. In the upper sixth, I became deputy head girl and house captain of Clairvaux. Each year, houses were expected to put on a short play and compete for a cup. In a class below me, a pupil called Anne Stallybrass was very good at acting and was always Herod in the nativity play. Anne then went on to a successful career on the stage and television, particularly her part as the wife of Captain Onedin in the eponymous series."

~~~~~~~~~~

PATRICIA LEWIS (née SHARPE) attended the school from 1952-54. She recalls:

"Madame Mildred was the headmistress. She was very strict, and discipline was high on the agenda at St. Bernard's.

"My best friend was Valerie Bachelor. We both enjoyed sport, our favourite being netball, followed by hockey. We also had the opportunity to play tennis on the courts opposite the school and occasionally go swimming. Once a week we were taken by bus, accompanied by Miss Johnson and Miss Haynes, to our sports field. It was something we all looked forward to, as we were free to play whatever sports we enjoyed most, or just run around the perimeter of the massive field.

"The uniform was a navy blue tunic which had the school badge and a school beret with a yellow tassel, or blue if you were a prefect. The uniform still sticks in my memory.

"In 1952, Princess Elizabeth became Queen Elizabeth II on the death of her father King George VI. On the occasion of her coronation in 1953, each child was given a book by Southend Borough Council entitled *The Crowning of the Queen*.

"All in all, my school days spent at St. Bernard's Convent were very, very happy indeed."

~~~~~~~~~~

Christine Britt (née Cotgrove) explains how the St. Bernard's Community made the school feel like one big family.

"There was a wonderful warmth about the building because it was truly a home with a fairly large and thriving community. Madame Vincent was a jolly, smiley nun who didn't teach, but helped with lunchtime duties and clubs. I can remember her tucking in her habit so that she could get down to playing table tennis with us. Mother Martin Mary was our maths teacher, known affectionately as 'The M. Squad', and Mother Gabriel used to run the tuck shop at break every day, selling the most delicious cream biscuits at a penny half-penny for three.

"Speech days were inspiring occasions with all pupils clothed in white dresses, socks and gloves. The school song was always sung with gusto and the front row of chairs in the hall taken up by governors in fox-fur stoles and impeccable suits, and the mayoral party resplendent in their chains of office.

"As the 1960s approached, Madame Mildred did warn us about these 'large music boxes' in cafes blaring out awful modern music. It was surprising then that we were allowed to hold 'Record Hops' during the lunchtimes in Lent to raise money for Africa. We were still in that politically incorrect era when 2s. 6d. bought 'a black baby'.

"One lasting memory, apart from the friendships made, is of the sound of footsteps from class after class descending the wooden stairs, with the piano playing in the hall, to line up, shortest first, tallest last, to attend assembly each morning, where we would be given news, sing a hymn and offer our day to God."

~~~~~~~~~~~

Margaret Tothill (née Curtois) attended St. Bernard's in the 1940s as a four-year-old, leaving when the younger students were moved to Lindisfarne. She returned to the school in the 1950s for her secondary education once she had left Lindisfarne. Throughout her time at the school she remembers:

"Madame Leonie, my first form mistress, recalled with great fondness, who dealt kindly with my tears on being parted from my mother.

"The pride I felt at completing the journey alone to school (when I was five) from Thames Drive to Milton Road by bus. The cost was 2d (two old pence) each way.

"I remember we had to curtsy individually to the Reverend Mother as we walked by her. This was replaced in later years by a respectful nod of the head.

"The gloom of being made to finish a bowl of tapioca and sitting in front of it all through playtime until lessons recommenced, sticks in my mind. I also remember the school had a dog; a large black Labrador called Rex.

"The supervision of school lunches from the stage in the hall by Madame Mildred whilst she read *The Times.*

"Taking part in the wonderful annual nativity play produced by Miss Angel, which had an amazing atmosphere of its own, and was always completely sold out.

"In terms of national events, I remember the 1951 general election when Churchill was re-elected. We were allowed to display Labour and Conservative political posters in our form room – quite surprising in retrospect."

~~~~~~~~~~~

GILL LEADBETTER remembers:

"There were Catholic and Protestant girls who had passed their 11-plus, and Catholic girls who had not. There were also girls from many other countries, including Anna Lavang from Vietnam who later became a nun.

"Quite a few of the girls in my class had gone to Lindisfarne, the preparatory school.

"Madame Mildred was a very gracious and, at the time I thought, old lady. She would glide across the hall from assembly, looking quite regal.

"We had diction with Miss Angel. Some of the girls had private diction and music.

"There were some wonderful school productions – the locally famous annual nativity play, and school house plays, and multilingual poetry reading competitions.

"When I was house captain in the late 1950s, our house,

Clairvaux won the house play competition, beating Fountains who had Helen Mirren as a performer.

"I think I was made a house captain with Madame Mildred's influence. She had told me she would fight tooth and nail to get me into college. I had messed up my 'O' levels and was doing a secretarial course in lower sixth which I hated. I ended up doing two years' work in one for 'A' level. The geography teacher, Miss O'Shaughnessey was a wonderful support.

"I went onto Goldsmith's and became a primary teacher and worked, mostly in London, for many years."

~~~~~~~~~~

Many of St. Bernard's ex-students have returned to the school as members of staff. **Carola Morton** was a pupil of St. Bernard's from 1952-59, where she was deputy head girl. She then returned to teach art in 1963 to 1965.

"I was in the final year at Lindisfarne when the King died. We were given the afternoon off school, so we could go to Victoria Circus to hear the proclamation of Elizabeth II as Queen.

"Many families bought TVs for the Coronation of Queen Elizabeth II. The screens were very small, often encased in mock wood, very expensive, took an age to warm up and were prone to all sorts of interference patterns, but we all longed to have one. On the great day, we dressed as far as possible in red, white and blue and I went to Elizabeth Gill's house in Leigh. Family, friends, neighbours and most of our form crowded in their living room. We really did understand it was a 'truly historic day', and we wrote essays about it for English and History for ages afterwards. Every pupil in the borough was given a coronation memento by the council. We secondary pupils received a book about royalty, and I wished I had been a year younger because primary pupils, like my brother, were given coronation mugs instead.

We wrote in ink, with dip-in pens. The desks we sat at had removable china ink-wells, periodically filled from a large metal jug with a long narrow spout. Only trusty pupils were allowed the job of ink-well filling, because it was very easy to miss, accidentally or otherwise, and spill ink through the desk hinge on to books stored inside. A particularly disliked punishment was collecting ink-wells after school and cleaning them out.

"Very few of us had a reliable fountain pen until the sixth form. Biros arrived in the mid-1950s, but were expensive, leaked badly and were definitely not allowed. Paper shortages after the war meant we were not allowed to waste any paper. Woe betides the pupil who tore a page out. Once, we tried to replace some torn out sheets with ones from an old exercise book, by carefully raising and replacing the staples. With a twinkle, Mother Vincent said she applauded the effort we had put in, even though we were clearly heading for hell and would be the death of her.

"In the immediate post-war years, meals were monotonous and largely horrible and we were not allowed to waste anything at all. For my first four years at St. Bernard's, we ate our meals in the school hall, sitting on benches at long trestle-tables. There was no choice of menu.

"One day there were squeals of horror because a great many ants had got into the vat of stewed apricots. The nuns did their best to say that we could leave the syrup with the ants in if we wished, though we should know that in some countries ants were regarded as delicacies, but we should eat the apricots themselves because they were good for us, and not make such a silly fuss.

"In our fifth year, the present on-site kitchen and dining room were built. We could sit round tables in groups on proper chairs, with proper crockery in a pretty shade of green, to serve ourselves with food that was actually enjoyable.

"We wore berets all year round. These were navy, with a small school badge on the front and medium blue tassel in the centre. We had blazers which we loved, but we had to wear navy coats in winter. We had to wear gloves to and from school. We knew that 'a lady would never eat in the street', and in uniform we never did. To this day I would feel uncomfortable doing so, except perhaps an ice cream on the seafront (beach side only). We were deeply trained. As pupils always will, we had many ways of customising our uniform. Our role-model was Brigitte Bardot, so we piled our hair up as artfully as we could, perching our berets precariously on top, secured with hat-pins, and clinched our waists in as tight as we could. In winter there was an optional navy sweater with double yellow stripes around the V-neck and cuffs. We always had to change our shoes from whatever we travelled to school in, which were supposed to be lace-ups in black or brown, to indoor ones which were usually brown sandals or white plimsolls. We stored the pair of shoes not being worn in a black shoe-bag, which we had to embroider with our name, and hang on our cloakroom peg.

"The words of the school song were regularly repeated to us: 'A child of St. Bernard's is known everywhere' and much as we laughed at it, we absorbed its message.

"In the 1950s, there was a large lawn, surrounded on two sides by a gravel path, alongside the hall. We used to have huge skipping games all along the path.

"As pupils always will, we did try to beat the system and we would exploit any loophole that presented itself. Sometimes our sense of humour led us astray. Once, when awaiting one of the Belgian nuns for a French lesson in a top-floor classroom, we decided to hide in the long cupboards under the eaves. The presence of the whole class crammed in there was revealed by our stifled giggles. Severe misbehaviour resulted in being sent to Mother Mildred. She had rather protruding eyes, and we believed one of them to be a glass one, though opinions differed as to which one it was, as they both seemed to have independent movement. Her gaze, which would have unnerved the most hardened of criminals, reduced us to tears in an instant.

"Mother Mildred was an amazing woman and, in a teaching career of nearly forty years, I never again knew a head teacher with her encyclopaedic memory of every pupil, past and present, and their families, her shrewd but caring sense of humour and her love of learning, her extreme wisdom and quiet kindness, and her patience, not to mention her sweetly Machiavellian tactics and the little smile she had when successful in them, as ultimately she usually was. She remains the perfect role-model for any teacher, and inspired my whole career.

"I owe a huge debt to the staff there at the time too, many of whom had taught me, and all of whom were quite surprisingly forgiving of the many hard times I had given them."

~~~~~~~~~~

MONICA BARNES attended the school from 1954 to 1958. She states:

"The school and the surrounding area were very different then.

"I entered St. Bernard's from St. Helen's primary school, which was then located next door to St. Helen's Church. The lay-out of St. Bernard's has changed so much over the years, with the nuns leaving and their quarters being used as classrooms.

"However, in essence it has remained the same; a place that nurtures both the academic and the spiritual. It is for this reason that I was very happy at St. Bernard's, and I am pleased to say that when my granddaughter comes to the school in September 2009, she will be the third generation of women in our family to attend the school."

~~~~~~~~~~

The physical education department, spoken of so fondly, have also contributed their memories to the book. MRS M. CONNELLY (née JOHNSON) and MRS M. WALMSLEY (née HAYNES) were staff at the school, 1949 to 1958. They remember that:

"At this time the Bernardine nuns were known as Madame followed by a chosen Saint's name. This was quickly changed when, at assembly, Madame Mildred announced that, following the summer break in France, all the nuns had become 'Mothers'.

"Developments in the P.E. department were exciting, as facilities and new innovations were being introduced in the aftermath of the Second World War. This began with a 'brightening up' of the school uniform – gold braid on the blazers and gold tassels on berets for prefects – blue tassels for the rest. These were compulsory, but obviously snatched off heads when past the school gates.

"The fairly modern well-equipped gymnasium was always in full use, with the main excitement of 'pirates' at the end of term, which comprised a chasing game on all the available surfaces. There was great emphasis on 'posture', for which badges were awarded and, together with early morning sessions of exercises to improve minor postural deformities, we hoped that we were making a difference.

"A specialist ballet teacher, Miss Blelloc, was already established in the curriculum. The department introduced National dance, particularly Scottish (popular in schools at the time) and ballroom dancing.

"Netball and hockey were the two main winter team games, with school matches being played on Saturdays. The department also ran a local school's league, with matches being played after school during the season when light prevailed. St. Bernard's netball team were not popular with their opponents when they won every match. This was due to playing three pairs of identical twins and Joan Perrot as centre. These were chosen from the Collins/Haywards/Quilters/Wightwicks. A successful annual tournament was held, usually at a school with more than one court.

"On one occasion, a group was taken to the Albert Hall to see a gymnastic display, in an 'off-the-road London Taxi', owned and driven by Miss Johnson. Miss Haynes was sitting on a box beside the driver, in the open luggage space, six girls tucked safely inside the cab – Health and Safety.

"The annual trip to Wembley to see the England women's hockey team was another highlight.

"The biggest adventurous event was the first skiing trip to Fiss, Austria. We were all gathered at Southend railway station for departure on Boxing Day morning on route via Harwich and onward by train. We set off without one of the group, who had forgotten that it was Sunday rail timetable. On arrival at Harwich, we were met by an announcement that Rosemary O'Brien would be travelling on her own. We were delighted when she arrived at the mountain village, having had an amazing journey – in her own words: 'I was treated like a Queen'. The weather was ideal; skiing progressed even with the instructors' limited English. Bridget Dixon was, unfortunately, hospitalised with pneumonia and kidney infection. As this was towards the end of the trip, Miss Haynes stayed behind with Pamela Stevens to assist, and Miss Johnson arrived home safely with the rest – some with minor injuries. The patient recovered enough to return on a stretcher and by air, with her attendants two weeks later.

"A great deal had to be packed into the summer term. Tennis and rounders were the main summer sports, culminating with the ever popular rounders match – pupils v. staff in fancy dress. Track events were already taught. At this time field events were not taught

The ski resort at Fiss; the destination of the first St. Bernard's ski trip

in any of the local girls' schools. Our school introduced javelin and discus. Very soon, interested schools followed.

"Swimming lessons were held at the Westcliff outdoor pool (now the site of the Westcliff Casino). Classes walked from school, down the cliffs and back in all weathers.

"The indoor pool at the Bernardine Prep. School at Lindisfarne was used by the department for a weekly swimming club. It was, therefore, possible to form a swimming team and, together with a tennis team, we were able to accept invitations from the Bernardine schools in France to compete in their galas and tournaments. We had an exciting match at the Mother house in Lille, trying to umpire tennis in French.

"During the summer term, visiting French nuns would accompany us on the school bus to the sports field, always so interested in the activities. On other occasions, there were incidents on the upper deck which heralded screams. One when the windows on one side were ripped out by overgrown trees, one sheet of glass having fallen behind Maureen Knight – no injuries. On another memorable trip, screams again. A pigeon had flown through the open window and landed with a broken neck on Mary Collins' lap.

"The department was also responsible for first aid, which included one first aid box and a rest room with a simple bed and army blankets. This was mainly used as a safe place for Helen Cleave's cello. The school's first aid treatment was highly praised by Southend A&E Department for very efficient bandaging by Miss Haynes. Ann Thompson decided to fly down the corridor straight through the domestic science glass doors, leaving the complete impression of her body. Fortunately, she was looking behind her, presumably at her chaser, but she cut both legs very badly.

"The department also ran part one of a pre-nursing course, in which the skeleton 'Adam' played an important part in the tuition, except when it was in fancy dress.

"The year culminated in the prize-giving ceremony, for which there were countless practices of stage seating arrangements, some standing on tiers of wobbly dinner benches and gym forms. On the day, with the Bishop, governors and visitors installed, the stage curtains opened to reveal a mass of pupils in white dresses and gloves – a sight to behold. Altogether this was a very happy and eventful era."

~~~~~~~~~~

The staff v. students netball match in 1956, in which the staff sported some colourful 'injuries'. Monica Hart and Ena Edwards are assisted by a school 'nurse'

A half-time photograph taken during the above netball match

The following memories were recalled in a telephone conversation between two old friends: (**Jean Burrow** (née Sibley) and **Sue Glassock** (née Sothcott) who works at the school today:

S: "Hi Jean, you know it's the school centenary next year? What can you remember about our time there?"

J: "Film Club, after school in the hall."

S: "The old Hall is now the Library."

J: "The films I remember are *Bambi*, *Carve Her Name with Pride* and the one about Douglas Bader, I forget what it was called."

S: "*Reach for the Sky*."

J: "And Mother Vincent's money-making schemes – lemon ice-cube lollies, little Japanese pencil tops and Lenten alms."

S: "She was always chasing us out of the Milton Road cloak-room at break-times."

J: "I remember speaking French with Mother Josephine; there always seemed to be French girls at the school, and later Vietnamese and girls from the Congo."

S: "I remember walking in a 'crocodile' to Lindisfarne in Valkyrie Road for swimming. It's now a snooker hall and leisure club."

J: "I remember swimming galas at Westcliff pool on the sea-front."

S: Yes, that's now a casino."

J: "First year Christmas party – girls only."

S: "Ballroom dancing lessons with Miss Blelloc. She taught us that 'girls at a dance should sit with knees together, hands on lap and always gracefully accept any invitation to dance, however unattractive your partner, and thank him afterwards'."

J: "Ice-cream and double break for Reverend Mother's Feast Day. Also, games in most of the lessons on St. Patrick's Day."

S: "Days off for Annunciation etc. And the priest always came to see the nuns on a Friday."

J: "I remember lots of competitions, inter-house games and plays, verse speaking, French verse speaking. Do they still have Houses?"

S: "Yes – and there's an extra one, A for Annay."

J: "Speech Day, with white frocks and gloves."

S: "Singing *All in the April Evening* and the school song."

J: "Yes, and hair to be plaited if it reached your shoulders. No nail varnish. Do you remember that, if you had it on, you were sent to the chemistry lab to have it removed with acetone."

S: "The same rule applies today."

J: "And definitely no make-up."

S: "That does creep in sometimes today."

J: "Do you remember swapping scarf tassels with girls from other schools?"

S: "Oh yes. The best ones were Westcliff High and St. Hilda's because of their colours."

J: "How about the hats?"

S: "Felt hats, navy berets with pale blue tassels and straw boaters in the summer."

J: "How about making the patchwork in needlework?"

S: "The girls still do that now."

J: "And knitting in maths lessons."

S: "Why did we do that? We don't any more."

J: "Nativity plays with Helen Mirren in the starring role."

S: "Yes, and elocution lessons with Miss Angel –

'The centipede was happy, quite, until the toad in fun said, pray, which leg goes after which? Which vexed his mind to such a pitch, he lay distracted in a ditch, considering how to run'."

J: "What about the school magazine – I still have one."

S: "So do I."

J: "What about cookery with Miss Pyecraft (good name for a cookery teacher)."

S: "I still have the recipes for baked stuffed fish, pork pies and American frosting – delicious."

J: "What about us writing all sorts of things on the inside of our satchels?"

S: "Yes, like 'a rolling stone gathers no moss, but it does gain a certain polish'."

J: "Yes, and 'Caesar adsum iam forte, Pompeii aderat, Caesar sic in omnibus, Pompeii sic innat'."

S: "Who wrote that chemistry lab poem? Was it Linda Ross?"

J: "'Little bottles in a row; taps containing H_2O'."

S: "Learning to touch-type to music with a wooden guard over the keyboard so you couldn't see the keys. It worked too."

J: "Oh, they were happy days weren't they?"

S: "Yes, they were – and still are."

A joint sixth form and staff party in 1959.
All participants had to design and make their own 'party hat'

Chapter 6

St. Bernard's in the 'Swinging Sixties'

HISTORICAL CONTEXT

1960	John F. Kennedy elected President of the United States
1961	The Berlin Wall erected
1962	Cuban Missile Crisis
1963	John F. Kennedy assassinated; The Beatles perform in Southend
1964	Nelson Mandela sentenced to life imprisonment in South Africa
1965	Winston Churchill dies
1966	England win the football World Cup at Wembley
1967	First 'successful' heart transplant performed in South Africa. The recipient lived for just eighteen days
1968	Martin Luther King assassinated in the United States
1969	Neil Armstrong becomes the first man to walk on the moon

~ 1960-1969 ~

ST. BERNARD'S DURING THE 'SWINGING SIXTIES'

During the 1960s, the school continued its expansion. In 1960, first-floor classrooms were added to the west wing and, in 1961, the second floor was added. In September of 1961, Sister Marie Mildred retired as headmistress, being succeeded by Sister Mary Aelred.

In 1966, Sister St. Michael replaced Sister Mary Aelred as headmistress. However, due to ill health, Sister St. Michael was unable to perform her duties, and Miss E O'Shaughnessy became acting headmistress.

The chapel underwent changes to reflect the changing times following Vatican II. The altar was moved forward so that the priest could face the people, and the tabernacle was placed in a niche behind the altar.

In 1967, a new organ arrived, followed by a new altar, courtesy of Mr. Wheeler, a school contractor.

In 1968, Lindisfarne Preparatory School closed, as other Catholic primary provision was now deemed adequate.

The 1960s were a time of great upheaval nationally, and some of the excitement and developments of that period were experienced by the students at St. Bernard's. For example, several letters commented on the impact of the Beatles coming to town. Southend was then very definitely on the circuit for the big acts of the day, with Roy Orbison, the Beatles, Gerry and the Pacemakers etc., all playing here.

1969 saw the first Moon landing, and this event was celebrated in the school library with a display of models, made by the students, of the lunar module and Apollo spacecraft.

During this period, preparations were underway for the school's Diamond Jubilee. The Jubilee committee organised several events, such as a Grand Firework Party, raffles, a fête, a sponsored walk and a Jubilee dance.

MEMORIES OF THE 1960s

ANNETTE FORKIN (née RICHARDSON) has many memories of her time at St. Bernard's:

"I started at St. Bernard's in September 1964, along with my best friend, Camilla Owen (whose sister, Penny, was already at the school). Excitement, mixed with trepidation, is my main memory of the occasion – and there are some sights, sounds and smells that stay with me to this day:

"My interview: firstly with Sister Mary Aelred, then with Miss O'Shaughnessy – not knowing whether, as a non-Catholic, I would be granted a place at the school;

"I remember going with my parents to buy my uniform at Perrings (now a wallpaper shop), on the corner of Milton Road; the inside dark, with polished wood drawer units, glass-topped counters, an elderly salesman who seemed to know all about what was needed for the school: cream blouses, navy knife-pleated skirt, jumper, tie, blazer, top-coat, gabardine, velour hat for the winter, boater and white gloves for the summer, science overall, art overall, outdoor shoes, indoor shoes, grey stockings, white socks – a huge wardrobe of new clothes;

"Arriving on my first day and lining up in the playground, according to our surnames; looking in awe at the older girls, who seemed so grown-up;

"My first sight of the cloakroom and the long, lino-covered corridor, the stone stairs to the right, at the bottom of which the tuck shop would be sited at break times – dear Mother Vincent standing by it, rattling her 'Congo Box' and making us feel all the more guilty about buying a Mars bar, or four ginger crunch biscuits for two (old) pennies;

"The buzzer, which would ring at times, when Miss O'Shaughnessy would summon one or more girls to her room, for some unknown misdemeanour;

"The school canteen where, at tables of six (four younger girls and two older girls serving), we gabbled through grace (very naughty), then had to finish everything before we were allowed to leave (hands up for a teacher to come and inspect the plates and serving dishes). Favourite desserts were chocolate pudding, steamed jam roll, chocolate crunch and milk jelly; not such favourite food, meat pudding and cabbage – all eaten as quickly as possible in order to dash out and bag the best tennis court.

"The teachers – all of whom I remember so clearly – our first form mistress, Miss Morris (who taught geography), Sister Mary Joseph (and later Miss O'Riordan) for maths, Mrs. Wade (and later Mrs. Greaves, then Sister Mary Stephen) for French, Sister Martin Mary for R.I., Miss Peel for history, Mrs. West for biology, Mrs. Foster for physics and chemistry, Mrs. Spary for music, Miss Wright, who played the piano for choir practice and as we filed out of the hall after assembly, Mrs. Lewis for needlework, Mrs. Welding and Miss Connelly for English, Miss Rigg (and later Mrs. Spavin) for German, Miss Thomas and Mrs. Adelarde for games, Miss Russell for speech training, Miss Blelloc for ballroom dancing (which we all loved) and of course Miss O'Shaughnessy, whose specialist subject was geography – of all the teachers, she especially was held in awe by all the girls.

"I soon made lots of new friends and settled into life at St. Bernard's quickly. It was a strict environment in those days – no running, no talking in the corridors, absolutely no eating sweets out-side school (I remember being told off by a couple of prefects for eating on my way home) – but nonetheless a very caring one. I enjoyed all my time there and forged friendships that have lasted many years.

"A few more memories from my mental scrapbook:

Speech days – all in our white dresses and white gloves, feeling terribly smart and grown-up;

"Hockey practice (having no playing fields, we had to bus over to St. Thomas More), freezing cold pitch, air so icy that it hurt to breathe, then tournaments against other schools, with the inevitable half-time oranges and three cheers for the winners (and losers) at the end of each match;

"A school trip to Paris, where we stayed at a school (empty because of their school holidays) and slept in a dormitory obvious-ly meant for much younger children (rubber under-sheets, ducks round the walls), early morning milky coffee out of huge bowls, wonderful French bread, trips to the Eiffel Tower, the Louvre, Notre Dame, Montmartre and the Sacre Coeur, the bouquinistes on the Left Bank, Galleries Lafayette, Versailles – all supervised by Mrs.

Greaves and Miss Newman (who insisted that we wear our school berets at all times, so that we could be easily spotted, and so drilled into us the dangers of the Paris metro – the doors that close and can trap you – that we were scared to death of going on it);

"Another trip – to Berlin this time (in 1970), where we stayed with individual families (I was with a Swiss scientist and his wife and three children, all of whom spoke wonderful English, so my German did not improve much) – the journey there by boat (very rough and lots of people feeling very queasy) and couchette (guards with dogs getting on as we crossed into East Germany, demanding passports and tickets);

"The freezing cold weather (snow in March); looking through the 'wall' at Wannsee where I stayed (at this location, this consisted of a double stretch of high barbed-wire fencing, patrolled by guards); visiting East Berlin via Check Point Charlie, seeing the very sparsely stocked shops, and eating venison in a large, dark hotel; loving West Berlin, with its wonderful shopping streets, open-air ice rink, nightclubs, museums, art galleries, theatres and concert halls – then the journey back, just as tiring as the one out, but with wonderful memories to take home;

"The Old Time Music Hall production we staged in 1969. This was huge fun, and raised lots of money for charity;

"House plays and winning the annual competition with George Bernard Shaw's *Passion, Poison and Petrifaction* when I was captain of Rievaulx in 1970-71 (this made up for coming last in the house sports competition);

"'Friendship Incorporated' – a scheme whereby girls would visit an elderly person, to keep them company – Val and I would go once a week to see Miss White, who lived in Shorefield Road and provided sandwiches and cakes for tea (and tea made with sterilised milk), in return for us playing duets with her on the piano;

"Fashions – Twiggy, Mary Quant, mini-skirts, the introduction of tights (hooray, no more suspender belts), platform shoes and boots, flower power and hippies;

"Music, the Beatles, the Rolling Stones, the Who, the Beach boys, Woodstock;

"TV – the first series of *Monty Python*; *TW3* with David Frost, Millicent Martin etc.;

"Politics – Harold Wilson as P.M.; the Common Market question; the proposal for comprehensive schooling; the death of Winston Churchill; the Vietnam War; the terrible disaster in Aberfan; England winning the World Cup, and the Moon landings. Looking back, so much was happening while I was at St. Bernard's that, in many ways, the school was the only constant in a changing world and it is good to know that it continues to provide the same supportive environment to those lucky enough to attend it now. In the words of the School Song; 'Long may St. Bernard's reign'."

~~~~~~~~~~

URSULA BARTLETT (née TAYLOR) has very vivid memories of her first day of school:

"On a chilly day, early in September 1964, I became a first year student at St. Bernard's in Westcliff, in Form I.3. I remember the large gates and the high walls surrounding the school. The grounds seemed vast, compared with the rather cramped surroundings I had experienced at St. Helen's School, which was then next door in the grounds of St. Helen's Church.

"First impressions – a haunting aroma of furniture polish, the grand wooden staircase and a certain 'presence' that I can still recall quite easily today. Mother Aelred, the headmistress, seemed very scary. 'Did the nuns have legs or hair?' we wondered, as the style of habit worn then revealed nothing, and they seemed to glide rather than walk along the corridors.

"Who could forget 'Mother V' (Sister Mary Vincent) with her Congo Box, always collecting for those less fortunate than ourselves. She ran 'Crusaders', a club which I joined, and we would make calendars to raise money. I wonder if anyone still has one of those masterpieces. Recycling Christmas cards was going on in St. Bernard's long before it became fashionable.

"During Lent, a few of us would try to attend Mass with the Sisters in the school chapel at 7.15am, as often as possible. One year my sister, Joan, and I managed to do this almost every school day. The reward, apart from the obvious grace received, was breakfast provided by the nuns."

~~~~~~~~~~

CAROLE SYMONS started St. Bernard's in 1963. She says:

"We were taught maths by Miss O'Connor. She always wore the full black gown and would sweep into the room with a great deal of presence, despite being quite short. It was April 1st, April Fools' Day, and we had decided that Miss O'Connor was to be a victim. We furnished ourselves with a small piece of material with a small snip in it. The moment she gathered her gown to sit down, we all ripped the fabric. There was a wonderful tearing noise and poor Miss O'Connor shot into the air.

"On one occasion towards the end of my first year at the school, I had gone to watch a rounders tournament that had been taking place on the grass. A rounders ball is not a soft object; the one that hit me in the eye was made of wood, covered in leather, and hurt a great deal. It smashed my glasses, and I was out cold on the ground. Sister Mary Edmund picked me up bodily and carried me into school. I was only twelve, in pain, in shock and in tears. Was I sent home? Were my parents contacted? Not at all. I was sent back to class and told to get on with it, in no uncertain terms, by my French teacher. The days of 'Health and Safety' and 'Duty of Care' were a long way ahead.

"When we went to the hall for assembly, we went in 'gym line'. This meant that the shortest were always at the front so everyone could see. I was one of those with restricted height, so I had an excellent view of the stage. During assembly, the staff would stand on the stage watching us. One morning, we noticed that one of the staff was very strangely attired. Mrs. Miller had her skirt on upside down and inside out. It was a straight, pull-on skirt, with no zip, so an easy mistake to make. The elastic was round her knees and the seams and labels were on show. We were convulsed.

"Eventually one of the staff noticed the problem and told her. She disappeared into the rooms behind the stage and 'adjusted her dress'. Sadly, I'm probably the age she was then, so I can understand how it happened.

"My last memory was again when I was in my first year. I was having piano lessons with Mrs. Spary. The music room was at the top of the new block. The block was linked to the old building via a short staircase from the top floor to the science labs. I waited for Mrs. Spary to come. A bell rang and, as we had staggered lunches, it was no surprise to me when all the seniors in the other classrooms filed out. Still I waited, and still no sign of Mrs. Spary. Then I heard a lot of noise outside and decided to look out of the windows. The entire school was on the playground. The bell I had assumed was the senior lunch bell was in fact the fire bell, and I was missing. A small fire had broken out in one of the labs, I think. When registers were taken, I obviously didn't answer and nobody knew where I was, until I appeared at the window."

~~~~~~~~~~

Christine Robson remembers her time at the school:

"My first year at the Convent was Madame Mildred's last year as headmistress. She had been the headmistress since before my mother attended the school thirty years previously. Such was her memory, she remembered not only my mother, but her two cousins as well.

"I remember my awestruck wonder at the nativity plays produced by Miss Angel. I think she left in my second or third year, and I don't recall anything else produced on such a scale whilst I was at the school.

"Deportment, elocution and ladylike behaviour were considered very important. I recall a stern lecture from Sister Aelred one assembly, where she exhorted us to use the more ladylike 'dearie me' instead of some rather more vulgar terms, which members of the public had reported hearing from St. Bernard's girls. For days after that, girls were heard around school saying 'dearie me' at every available opportunity, but I think we got the message. After all, 'A child of St. Bernard's is known everywhere.'

"It was the 'Swinging Sixties', and mini-skirts were in fashion, but at St. Bernard's, your skirt had to touch the floor when you knelt down. We girls used to turn our skirts several times at the waist, only to let them down again quickly when we observed a nun or other strict member of staff approaching along the corridor.

"Several of my friends and I were members of the Gerry and the Pacemakers' Fan Club. One lunchtime, a friend and I were eagerly perusing the latest edition of the fan club magazine. So engrossed were we that we didn't hear the whistle calling us in to afternoon school. Eventually, the extreme quietness around us must have alerted us to the fact that we were on our own in the playground. Unfortunately, I cannot remember the excuse we gave to the teacher to account for our lateness.

"Everyone said that our form was the naughtiest in the school (they probably said that to every class). However, we did pull off some amazing stunts. On one occasion, when we were supposed to be leading into assembly, the girl at the front of the line led the whole class, lined up in height order, right through the hall and out the other end. Imagine the incredulous looks on the faces of the staff assembled on the stage as we marched solemnly past them. We got a class detention for that.

"On another occasion, our Latin class hid from Mrs. Miller in the second of the two rooms at the top of the stone staircase. The poor lady climbed the stairs several times looking for us. She was none too pleased, and the test from which we had been trying to escape was even harder as a consequence.

"In case you are wondering whether we ever did any work; despite our boisterous ways and harmless pranks we studied hard, and I often did three or four hours homework a night. I found maths particularly difficult, and it is thanks to Miss O'Connor that maths was one of the seven 'O' levels I had gained by the end of the fifth year.

"I have many other memories which would probably fill a whole book but for now I must close. Thank you St. Bernard's, 'Long may she reign'."

~~~~~~~~~~

ALISON HILLIER attended the school from 1964-1969:

"My first form mistress was Mother Mary Joseph, who also taught me maths and R.E. I was in the choir and took part in the Southend Music Festival and was also form captain.

During the third and fourth years, I was in the drama club, and in the summer of 1968, I played Hortensio in a cup winning performance of *The Taming of the Shrew*.

"I have many fond memories, including learning to ballroom dance and always having to be the boy as I was so tall; needlework classes and the nightdress I made, which looked like a barrage balloon when I'd finished it; the swimming gala, where I was in the walking race as I couldn't swim; and being concussed by a discus and throwing up in Miss Lawton's car when she took me home.

"I enjoyed my school days very much and can't believe where the years have gone."

~~~~~~~~~~

GILLIAN GRAY (née HOSKEN) remembers the effect of a national event on St. Bernard's:

"It was October 1962. The news was grim. The Cuban missile crisis had brought the world to the brink of nuclear war. In lower sixth we were deeply worried: it could mean the end of the world. But when we confided in Mother Aelred, the elderly nun who taught us Latin, she had no such fears.

"Striding to the classroom door she declared, in the northern accent she never lost despite her many years in Westcliff: 'This, girls, is where the world began.' Taking a few steps into the classroom, she went on: 'In 1962 we are here, this is as far as the world has got. Only when it reaches that window, over there, will it end.' We were all completely reassured and, within days, Mother Aelred's faith was proved correct. The Soviet leader, Nikita Khrushchev, promised to dismantle Soviet missiles based in Cuba, and President Kennedy agreed to lift the U.S. blockade of the island and promised that the U.S.A. would not invade Cuba. Perhaps the two super-power leaders had heard Mother Aelred's prayers.

"Mother Aelred helped us to keep things in perspective. I remember how, when faced with our mounting worries over our G.C.E. exams, she reminded us: 'When he goes down on his knees to ask you to marry him, he's not going to demand to know, first of all, if you got Latin 'O' level.'

"There was never any suggestion, however, that, as girls, all we could aspire to was marriage and a family. We were constantly encouraged to get the best results we could, to get good qualifications and to go on to have a career or a fulfilling job.

"My mother always believed that the nuns gave us a feeling of security. People like Mother Alix, our first form teacher, Mother

Vincent (Mother 'V') who, every break-time, was to be found sell-ing trinkets from our school in Japan, or St. Christopher medallions, or home-made ice lollies.

"I hope today's girls get as much from St. Bernard's as I did. I'm grateful to the nuns and to teachers like Miss O'Shaughnessy, Mrs. Greaves, Mrs. Black and, of course, Miss Angel (the mastermind behind the nativity play) for the education I had and for seven years of friendship and happiness at St. Bernard's."

~~~~~~~~~~

SVETLANA TONIC (née CUBRILO) shares her memories:

"I passed the 11-plus and my wonderful mama had already decided – St. Bernard's was going to be our choice.

"My parents were political immigrants, having been against com-munism during the Second World War. They were on a death list to be shot – my mother was fifteen, my father seventeen. They finally arrived in Westcliff in the 1950s.

"My mama always said she would like her daughters to go to St. Bernard's. She loved the uniform and obvious discipline, and we would come out as ladies. Going to Hornes' Brothers in the High Street to buy my quite expensive uniform was an occasion. Every time friends came, I had to show off my uniform. I was very, very proud to wear that uniform. It stood for humility, truth, honesty, hard work and belief. My parents left their country, family and friends in order to hold onto these values, so St. Bernard's was an obvious choice.

"In the sixth form I was made games captain of the school and, before leaving, I was given the Tolhurst prize for being an 'example of a St. Bernard's girl' – what an honour for me and my family, especially my mama, whose dream I fulfilled with pleasure.

"I did receive £5 from Thames Television Wardrobe Department, after lending my school uniform to Helen Mirren to wear as she was filmed walking along Westcliff Beach in a docu-mentary on her life as a pupil of St. Bernard's. I got my uniform back."

~~~~~~~~~~

Lesley Hickson (whose account of a play in the early 1970s appears in Chapter 7) explains the concept behind the following photographs:

"These photos were taken in the summer of 1968 or 1969, in the days when you could roam free without the need to clasp a mobile phone. Each week, we would fix a meeting point near the home of one or another of us and set off armed with 'nosh, slosh and dosh' (food, drink and money).

"On this particular trip, we walked through some wet fields and decided to dry our socks off on a long branch, which was carried shoulder-high through various Essex villages. This was the only trip for which we had a camera and, after the picnic, we did a session of trick photography before heading home; not before posing around the sign post to show the location of our day out."

~~~~~~~~~~~

Trick photography taken on Ashingdon Hill in the days before digital manipulation. Caroline Curtis 'holds' Jo Burry, Arlene Bell, Catherine Friday, Lesley Hickson, Pip Hawkes and Linda Rothman on her hands

The same girls as on the previous page, drying their socks after a particularly wet walk

JUDITH GOODENOUGH was at the school from 1959-64. She has clear memories of the impact the Beatles had on St. Bernard's:

"The excitement when it was announced that the Beatles were coming was intense. We knew that tickets for the Beatles would be hard to get and we would have to queue for days before the box office opened – but how to arrange it during a school week?

"In shifts, of course. I was on one of the day shifts and took my place early one cold morning on the pavement alongside the Odeon – not that far from the front of the queue. Others, with more enlightened parents, would take over the evening and night shifts (with chaperones), and that way, we could buy the tickets we needed.

"The police patrolled the queue, checking all us young girls were OK, chatting to us and making remarks such as 'you'll get piles sitting down there,' and 'shouldn't you be at school?' and 'do your parents know you're here?'

"Soon we noticed adults coming towards us, checking the queue. Oh no; a teacher from Southend High. Quickly, we hid some near-

by girls under blankets and sleeping bags. Panic over – they didn't
see them. Then along came St. Bernard's teachers; the girls from
Southend High repaid the favour, and we escaped recognition too.
There must have been a lot of truanting in Southend for a few days.

"Yes, we got our tickets. Yes, we had great seats. Yes, the show
was fantastic. Yes, we screamed all evening. Yes, I'll never forget it."

Judith also remembers the following:
    "Mother Vincent and her whistle;
    "Turning up the waistband of your skirt after assembly;
    "Playing tennis in the park over the road;
    "Going by bus to play hockey in the freezing cold;
    "The school song;
    "The fire on the roof of the new art corridor;
    "Mother Vincent checking every line of your book was filled
before you got a new one;
    "Panama hats in summer (fabulous frisbees);
    "High jump and long jump in the nuns' garden;
    "The lorry carrying pigswill that passed under our window;
    "Pulling down the sleeves of your jumper whenever a nun was
in sight;
    "Lining up in height order for assembly;
    "The chapel;
    "A satchel full of homework every day;
    "Always organising the same eight girls at the dinner table;
    "The nativity plays and the beautiful singing;
    "Ballroom dancing lessons;
    "The first male teacher;
    "Mercury and Bunsen burners in the science labs;
    "Cutting up bulls' eyes and worms;
    "Sliding on the wooden floors in the corridor;
    "Watching the nuns hanging out their washing;
    "The huge tins of peaches outside the nuns' kitchen;
    "Prize giving;
    "The choir;
    "Sports days – and the competition between the houses:
Melrose, Fountains, Rievaulx and Clairvaux;
    "Struggling with Latin;

The chapel as it was when the Bernardine Order took over the school in 1910.
It was very much more elaborate than it is today.
The side altars have now disappeared, and there is a simple wooden altar in the centre

The reception area in the late 1920s and early 30s

The wooden staircase, which remains unchanged to this day

An early dormitory from the 1920s, when St. Bernard's was a boarding school

The dining room, situated in what is now a language room E03

A view of the science lab of the 1930s,
with the girls in their gymslips and white shirts with Peter Pan Collars

The school hall, possibly set up for examinations. The windows and doors are unchanged, but today the hall houses the library and computer suite

An early school trip from the 1920s. Most of the girls have berets with a school badge. Does anyone know where the trip was going? What a fabulous vehicle!

Madame Mildred standing in the old entrance to the school

UNIVERSITY OF LONDON

THIS IS TO CERTIFY that

Betty May Coakes

having at the General School Examination held
Midsummer 19*35* reached the standard required
for Matriculation in the following subjects—

English   *Elementary Mathematics*

History (English & European)   *Geography*

French   *Botany*   *Drawing*

matriculated in the University of London as from
January   193*7*.

S. J. Worsley

Acting Principal

An example of the certificates awarded for Matriculation.
Betty May Coakes, who provided this, matriculated from St. Bernard's in 1937

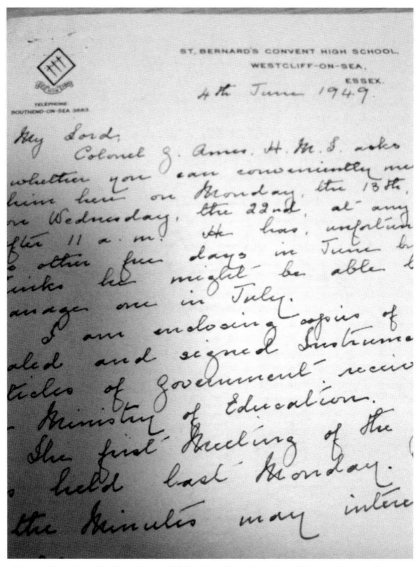

A letter from the school archive in 1949, when the school was facing a change of status

One of the school netball teams in 1959.
Patricia Stevens, Valerie Robbins and Leonora Willis are three of the members.
Notice the divided skirts and sashes which made up the P.E. uniform

Leonora Willis and Pat Newman with 'Adam', the school's skeleton,
who assisted in biology classes

Sister Marie Josephine (Reverend Mother) and Sister Marie Mildred (headmistress) photographed in front of the new canteen

The new kitchens built to feed the growing school community

Miss Claire Angel, the much-loved drama and speech training teacher, with her husband, Mr Chapman. She organised the famous nativity plays which so many remember

A group of St. Bernard's girls on a ramble in the 1960s. Sally Gloyne is on the signpost with, from L-R, Catherine, Caroline, Lesley, Arlene, Pip, Linda and Jo

Preparing to film Hiawatha in the nun's garden.
Josephine Burry (now Mrs Ronan) is Hiawatha

A letter from the archives which announces the retirement
of Madame Mildred as headmistress in 1962

ESSEX.

19th February, 19   .

TELEPHONE:
SEND-ON-SEA 43583.

JET/ER

My Lord Bishop,

    Madame Mildred is retiring as Head Mistress
of St. Bernards this summer and we shall be saying
farewell to her on Speech Day this year, which has
been fixed for the 21st July.

    As this will be a very special occasion, I
wonder whether it will be possible for you to
preside and in particular, join the school in thanking
Madame Mildred for all she has done for St. Bernards.

    Madame Mildred came to St. Bernards in 1912
and was appointed Head Mistress in 1924.

        Yours sincerely,

A view of the new sixth form block, officially opened in 1972.
Sister Mary Stephen is shown helping a student.
This is now the North Wing corridor, and houses maths classrooms

Madame Mildred and Reverend Mother with V.I.P. guests at the official opening of the
Diamond Jubilee Extension (The North Wing) in 1972

Madame Mildred, with the plaque commemorating the opening of the Jubilee Building

A view of the school after the Jubilee extension was added

A group of sixth formers at the official opening of the Jubilee building.
Anyone you recognise?

Important Events.

1st Year.   Form Prefect : Janice Swain   Rm.4
Japanese Lessons. (abandoned due to lack of interest!)
London Zoo 1st Year Science Trip.
Emma & Alison H. won carol contest.
Sally, Le-ee, Jackie entered our form.
Helen Colvert left.
Tate Gallery with S.M.M. (Exhibition for the Blind)
Geography trip to Hobbs Cross Farm.
'Oliver' (Maria in the title role)
Victoria in Thames Television London Quiz.

2nd Year.   Form Prefect   Shealagh Daubeny   Rm.2
Commonwealth Institute.
Hampton Court
The Mystery of the stolen Purse. (Winnie the Jet)
Josephine and Pauline entered our form.
Raised £75 for leprosy fund.
Debbie Smith Jones & Alison Price left.
'Trial by Jury'
Trip to 'Cinderella'
Emma broke the crucifix.

An extract from a pupil's scrapbook, showing the wide range of activities on offer

The winners of the National Public Speaking Competition organised by the English Speaking Union in 1982. The Lord Bailleau Trophy was awarded to Jill Murray, Sally Paviour and Simon MacCormac

An aerial view of the school in the 1970s, before the sports hall, arts building, multi-use games area and sixth form study centre were added

A staff pantomime, with Mrs. Mitchell in the centre

Cinderella, with Mr. Hind playing a starring role

Preparing to go onstage for *Guys and Dolls*

The leading men in *Guys and Dolls*

Jenny Gaynor, who played Adelaide in *Guys and Dolls*, with the dancers

A sixth form still-life drawing class, in what had been the nuns' kitchen,
and is now the sixth form common room

A group of Year 8s, suitably attired for their trip to Kentwell Hall.
The girls and teachers all made their own costumes

A Year 7 history trip to Southchurch Hall

The remains of the steel air raid shelters discovered under the playground during the building of the Bernardine Hall. They had been filled with rubble and forgotten

A strange find during the excavations of the air raid shelters

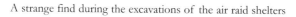

The official photograph of the St. Bernard's Football Team that won the National
Schools' Championship run by Coca-Cola, with the Mayor and Mayoress of Southend

A view of the new gardens laid out in 2008

The Memorial Arbour, erected in memory of Bill Sanders and Carolyn Lettieri

Part of the new landscaped gardens

The new gardens with performance area

A non-uniform day with a fancy dress theme in 2007

Year 13 history students, as they prepare to leave St. Bernard's, looking back to the past

A scene from *Oliver*. Hayley Stockwell as Oliver, and Megan Fanning as Fagin (2007)

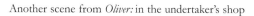

Another scene from *Oliver:* in the undertaker's shop

A scene from *Annie*, with Laura Marsden playing the title role (2009)

The cast of *Annie*

A group of present day students outside the school

The school as it looks today. Notice the new Reception and front doors

Helen Mirren, perhaps one of the most well known 'old girls' of St. Bernard's.
She attended the school in the early 1960s.
(photo courtesy of Giles Keyte)

"Learning a poem in detention (I still remember most of it);

"Not wanting to leave St. Bernard's ...;

"And, last but not least –;

"Those magnificent nuns who lived in the attic ..."

~~~~~~~~~~

FELICITY PAWSEY (née RAMSDEN) attended St. Bernard's 1966-70. She has many memories of the school, among which are:

"Assemblies: each class had to file in with everyone in height order. Being the smallest in my class, I was always in front and therefore never escaped the watchful eyes of the staff;

"The nuns' garden: a rectangular piece of lawned garden, to one side of the school, on which we had hurdles, long jump, high jump, javelin and discus. A statue of Our Lady watched over us. Rumour said that, when we'd all gone home, the nuns would come and have a go at the long jump etc., or else come down here to kick a ball around. I wonder if they did?;

"Swimming lessons held in the municipal open air swimming pool on the seafront in Westcliff. Freezing water and a brisk wind made it a far from pleasant experience;

"Being 'well brought up young girls', we had ballroom dancing lessons in the school hall;

"A warren of rooms, staircases and corridors, and, because it was home to the nuns, parts of the building were out of bounds. Notices on those doors read 'Community Only' and, although we speculated, we never got to see what went on behind them."

~~~~~~~~~~

PAULINE HUNTINGTON remembers the strict uniform rules at St. Bernard's:

"My career at St. Bernard's began in 1965, the year that also heralded the advent of the mini-skirt. While I struggled with details of long socks (grey in winter and white in summer), indoor and outdoor shoes, berets and straw boaters, Mary Quant was showing the women of the world another way to adorn themselves. Hemlines of eight inches above the knee were causing a sensation in 'swinging

London'. In not so swinging Westcliff, the pleated navy skirts of our uniforms were not permitted to settle any higher than an inch from the floor when the wearer was kneeling.

"A first-year student can be expected to follow the rules. By the second year, however, the rules are expected to be broken. Rolling up the skirt at the waistband was the universally accepted method. This temporary means of adjustment allowed us a more respectable 4-5 inches of above-the-knee flesh to be paraded before our peers, while a quick tug could have the skirt back to following the rules whenever a teacher came in sight.

"Straight-jacketed in uniforms that had to conform to rules more difficult to follow than the Ten Commandments, there was little scope for the creative imaginations of the pupils. The only other outlet (apart from the rolled-up skirt) for my classmates and I was provided by the school tie.

"Navy blue with thin yellow and light blue, diagonal stripes, the tie was to be tied in the conventional manner. The stripes, however, left room for invention. By tugging at and eliminating carefully selected threads, the lower end of the tie could assume patterns otherwise probably unthought-of and definitely unintended by the original designer.

"I think the restrictions placed upon us only served to further encourage creativeness and originality, and I look back on those days with fond memories."

~~~~~~~~~~

Wendy McCormick attended St. Bernard's after the Second World War, but returned in 1959 as a teacher. She states:

"Being the 1960s, women's rights were very much in people's minds. One of the nuns gave a talk once, and Mother Mildred gave out a card called 'The Rights of Women'.

The right to serve and love,
The right to sympathise,
The right to nurse the infant tenderly, to guide, teach, and warn,
The right to be awake when all are sound asleep,
The right to bring light to darkness,

The right to bear with patient love, the burdens and cares of others,

The right to believe firmly and to remain faithful when fearful doubts surge,

The right to forgive without number. In a word – the right to be entirely woman, full tender, good and true –

That is the most beautiful of all women-rights.'

"St. Bernard's was unique, with a great sense of community, underpinned by the prayers and devotion of the nuns. They had tremendous insight, which I think is reflected in their perspective on this subject."

~~~~~~~~~~~

FIONA SWERDLOW (née SIM) remembers her time at the School:

"I present here some memories from my time at St. Bernard's which I think are worth sharing:

"Throughout my St. Bernard's career (1965-72), we were told we were a 'good year', whatever that meant. Expectations were high, or relatively so. In the early 1970s, most St. Bernard's girls were expected to go directly into respectable employment, or to acquire secretarial skills, or to go to teacher training college or nursing school, with the remainder proceeding to university. So, when I declared that I wanted to apply to study medicine, I was gently advised by my teachers and advisers of the error of my ways, since this was not considered a sensible aspiration for a St. Bernard's girl at the time.

"Even at that time (prior to any discrimination legislation), I was disgusted by the discovery that some universities required higher 'A' level grades from girls than boys. I went on to study at my first choice, which was U.C.L. After my experience, as I was delighted to discover some years later, there had been a steady trickle of successful applications from St. Bernard's to study medicine, which was no longer 'out of bounds'.

"I was one of six Jewish girls in my year, the most ever recalled in a single year and therefore something of a novelty at the Convent School. We were encouraged to observe our religion. Woe betide any of the six who failed to stay away from school on a religious holiday. We were invited to demonstrate at school how the different festivals were celebrated. This was popular with everyone as it tended to involve time away from serious lessons, and sampling cakes and other edible delicacies for which Judaism is well known. The experience of mutual respect for people of diverse faiths engendered at St. Bernard's has always remained with me.

"When I was in the sixth form (1971-72), an exciting one-off was the production of *The Pirates of Penzance*, starring an all-girl cast and culminating in a highly successful performance, thanks to immense patience on the part of the staff concerned. Coming across a photo recently from that production of *Pirates* made me laugh out loud, as the memories of rehearsals and performances, not to mention make up and costume, flooded back."

~~~~~~~~~~

Josephine Ronan, (née **Burry**) attended the school between 1965 and 1972, and returned to the school as a teacher in the 1990s. She is now the head of history:

"The things that I remember most clearly are the productions that I took part in. We had a young P.E. teacher who introduced 'modern dance', and I remember rehearsing a whole dance sequence to *Who Will Buy?* from *Oliver*, which we performed at a Festival of Dance.

"I also remember putting on another dance, where I had a starring role. I was the cruel lover in *Puppet on a String*. I know some of my friends were not too happy about being part of the roundabout, but I loved my part.

"I also got to play Hiawatha in a film version that we made with our English teacher, Mr. Fretwell, in Year 3. It required me to dress up as an indian brave and do a lot of running.

"Another very clear memory is playing hockey in freezing cold weather on the fields at Bridgewater Drive. Someone made up a song about it (probably Sally Gloyne) to the tune of 'I love to go A-Wandering'. I still remember some of it:

'I love to go a-wandering across a hockey pitch,
But every other step we take lands us in a ditch,

Hit it on.

Blow its gone.

Down to the other end … etc'.

"Other things that stay in the memory are playing scrum on the field, making snowmen, the annual carol concert with nativity play and the house plays.

"Finally, I made good friends at St. Bernard's, some of whom I still keep in contact with today. We used to go out at weekend on long rambles. We explored the local areas, taking packed lunches and only having to return home at dusk. We had a wonderful freedom then that many girls do not seem to have today."

~~~~~~~~~~

Josephine Burry (now Mrs. Ronan) as Hiawatha.
The picture was taken by the slope in the nuns' garden

Theresa Whitaker (née Burry) is Josephine's sister and attended St. Bernard's from 1959-66:

"I remember: going down the staircase into the hall for assembly, with first years joining the school last, and all lines vertically down the hall, singing a hymn, then total silence and Madame Mildred in charge;

"Sixth formers taking younger classes into the hall for assembly. Our monitor was Christine Soper, and we were all a little in awe of her;

"Trying to catch a glimpse of the nuns' underwear hanging on the lines in the school courtyard;

"The day the world was supposed to end. During lunch break it started to rain and everyone started to squeal. Mrs Black told us not to be so silly;

"The Shakespeare Cup competition; all classes produced a piece from a Shakespeare play. The finalists performed in front of the school. The winners were usually the class containing Helen Mirren;

"The 'arty' group, so distinguished by their hair, short hitched up skirts and elite appearance;

"The Christmas productions led by Miss Angel, and the waft of perfume that followed her around the corridors;

"Having to learn poetry off by heart for Miss Angel for elocution lessons; *The Naming of Cats* by T. S. Elliot was the first poem we learned;

"The kindness of Sister Stephen when I was ill, letting me stay on after school to stay and catch up on missed lessons.

"The very small sixth form (about 22 in the upper sixth) being allowed to cook our own lunch in the cookery room. We were often visited by boys from Southend High – all members of I.S.A.S. (Inter School Arts Society);

"Queuing all night for the Beatles concert and getting tickets for the second row for myself and Maureen Daly;

"Country dancing at a school fete. A group of about six, wearing white with tartan sashes, dancing to the pipers, played by, I think, Mrs. Welding's son. We had to go to her house in Rochford to practise."

~~~~~~~~~~

CAROL SNELLING (née GUIVER) remembers a school trip during the 1960s:

"During a school visit to La Plaine in the spring of 1963, I climbed yet again over the sill of one of the windows at the château. I reflected that it had been a very unusual term so far. I had been promised up to a month in France over the Easter season but the Education Department extended this a further fortnight.

"The day had been daffodil bright, sparkling but very cold, and I had returned to the château to find a pullover and a warmer jacket. As I walked back, the quiet area had become shadowed and tense. I had walked right in before, across the road, balancing on the heavy wet cobbles and offered flowers by the local women that lingered there.

"But, today had been different; I had found five rifles pointed suddenly and directly at me, as the barrier into Belgium from Lambersat was unexpectedly closed. 'Where's your passport?' 'Have you enough food?' 'No bread to come through customs.' 'The mines have been shut, completely. Lille is at a standstill – the poor and the unprepared are already suffering.' 'Where are you going?'

"I was obviously not in Westcliff uniform; the château girls wore navy tabliers – my clothes in gentle English country colours had turned me into something else other that a St. Bernard's schoolgirl hurrying into La Plaine. Fortunately, a careful perusal of Koestler's *Le Lion* in the days before had helped my little French to explain, but not before the police were called.

"Sr. Mary Aelred, my Latin teacher, came later on another day, and when she heard about this she absolutely shrieked. She also told me, ironically, that they were going to need another head of French in the future.

"On the day of Princess Alexandra's wedding to Angus Ogilvy, I was joined at the Château de la Plaine by a very elderly nun who was practising her English. Together, we watched the ceremony on a tiny television, as we munched on salmon sandwiches."

~~~~~~~~~~

JUDITH LAWRENCE (née BURSTIN) remembers:

"An English lesson with Mr. Fretwell, which involved running along the cliffs with Josephine Burry, while we acted out and filmed *The Song of Hiawatha*. Jo was the eponymous Hiawatha. (Does this film still exist?);

"Being taken to see *Camelot* with another girl, as a prize in a poetry competition;

"Climbing over the gates at White City, led by Sister Mary Edward, when the original venue for the Ladies' England hockey finals, Wembley, was closed;

"The life-sized mermaid that I made for an art project, constructed of chicken wire, foil and cellophane. It lived in my garage for ten years;

"Playing scrum in the nuns' garden, and Miss Newbury hanging out of the art room window to tell us off;

"Mr McEwan's 'Mass equals weight over unit volume', in a purr of a Scottish accent (everyone had a crush on him);

"Someone singing off-key in Mrs. Greaves' French lesson. Mrs. Greaves demanded that the person who was off-key stop singing. When no one did, she split the group into two and made each group sing separately. This continued until, by a process of elimination, she finally unmasked the culprit, me. I was still singing at the top of my voice, completely unaware that I was not in tune with everyone else. It didn't stop me singing, but I do warn people first;

"An eventful holiday in Greece with Mrs. Miller; the shipping line was Egyptian, the accommodation double booked and the school given cabins below decks, reached only by walking through the crew's quarters. Mrs. Miller led her group of sixteen-year-old convent girls up to sleep on deck, rather than have them exposed to this;

"The 'O' level results were due, and I remember that one day on my way to the hotel, I was met by friends waving a telegram for me. Had my parents, despite strict instructions not to, sent my results? No, it was my boyfriend: 'Arsenal top of Division 1. Love Raymond'. It was the only telegram that I ever received. Another memory of this holiday was of a group of Greek boys following me and Mary O'Brien, asking 'You wanna go to a Deeskotea?' and offering cigarettes. Thirty years later, I received a postcard from

Athens, unsigned, with the message 'You wanna go to a Deeskotea?' It was Mary; we had been out of touch for twenty-five years."

~~~~~~~~~~~

VALERIE WILCOX (née POLLITT) has provided a lot of information about her days at St. Bernard's. One vivid memory is the 'Old Time Music Hall' musical which her class, 5.2, performed in 1969. It raised £22 10s. and included such classics as *Tip-toe through the Tulips, Daisy, If You Were the Only Girl in the World,* and *Down at the Old Bull and Bush.* Below is a photo of the girls involved:

The cast of the 'Old Time Music Hall' performed in 1969 by class 5.2.
They raised £22.10s. .0d

St Bernard's 2nd XI hockey team in March 1968:
Back row L-R: Maureen McKenna, Maureen Furley, Beverley Shepherd,
Carol Lewis, Maria Ross, Valerie Pollit.
Front Row L-R: Susan Carter, Christine Murray, Annette Richardson,
Janice Salmon, Sandra Jeckells

Valerie was also in the St. Bernard's Hockey 2nd XI team, whose picture appeared in the *Southend Standard* in March 1968. Valerie also sent in a project completed in 1971 in which she had recorded the history of the school. This has been very interesting and useful.

~~~~~~~~~~

HELEN MIRREN attended the school in the 1960s. She has since gone on to star in many productions, both on stage and screen:

"One of my strongest memories of St. Bernard's is olfactory; the smell of a lovely combination of lavender floor polish and incense. That tells you that, when I attended the school, it was home to a community of Bernardine Sisters, who glided around the halls in their distinctive black gowns and very white wimples, starched to a sharp crispness that was like card paper. Their washing line, discreetly hidden behind a fence, was a subject of great fascination to us pupils, with its mysterious pieces of oddly shaped linen. There was a tiny patch of grass with some trees and bushes around it, just below the playground/tennis/netball court known as 'the nuns' garden', and this was where the nuns could be seen, sometimes circling in pairs, fingering their rosaries in silent prayer.

"It was much later that it dawned on me that this was an enclosed order and this little patch of garden was where the sisters meditated, rested and took their recreation. Later still, I was shown into the tiny bedrooms where those nuns who taught us, and who polished the floors, kept us girls in order and, I'm sure, prayed for us, lived (sometimes two to a room); it was then that I came to understand their special sense of service and dedication to the religious life they had entered.

"Although my parents were not Catholic (in fact, not religious at all), the grammar school in St. Bernard's was considered to be the best in the neighbourhood, and my parents fought hard to get my sister and I a place. It provided a good academic education for us, especially in the arts, even then. The science and physics teachers, however, were sometimes driven to distraction and despair by the intellectual resistance they encountered in general, exacerbated by antiquated equipment and poorly supplied rooms.

"However, I left St. Bernard's having learnt two languages, three if you count Latin, and also with a love of maps and geography, instilled by a terrifying but lovely teacher, Miss O'Shaughnessy, who later went on to become head teacher at the school. I had a marvellous maths teacher for a year, and I shot up the class; sadly the following year she moved on, and I fell back into the fog I had lived in before, as far as maths was concerned. This is a clear example of the power of a good teacher. We also had a great arts teacher in Mrs. Campbell, and a new art room wing in which we could do great big sploshy paintings.

"In English literature, I had the great fortune to be taught by a truly wonderful teacher Mrs. Welding, who enlightened and excited everyone she taught. It was Mrs. Welding who told me about the National Youth Theatre and launched me on the path that has brought me to where I am now.

"However, this was an exception because, in general, at St. Bernard's at that time, there was little encouragement of ambition as, in the Catholic tradition, our destiny was felt to be wives or mothers. If you had to work, 'be a nurse or a secretary, preferably in the Civil Service,' was the extent of careers advice. We were taught the skills of a nicely brought up young lady: how to make a pillowcase by hand, with teeny weeny stitches; history according to Catholic understanding and the words to Elizabethan songs. If your parents desired, you could pay extra for elocution lessons with the wonderful Miss Angel (whom I adored because of her expertly applied false eyelashes – so glamorous).

"Uniform was deemed to be of huge importance, with appointed prefects trying to keep us all in line. There were endless rules about how to wear it: at what angle the hat should be; how long the skirt should be worn and how many buttons needed to be done up.

"The St. Bernard's I remember was clearly very different from the school of today, with its vibrant inhabitants, diverse curriculum and classrooms full of equipment. However, there is still a spirit there that has remained, maybe instilled by the memory of the nuns, swishing down the polished wooden floors. I like to think that it is a sense of the ongoing belief in optimism, decency and an education that is not just about academia but also about how you live your life."

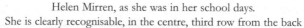

Helen Mirren, as she was in her school days.
She is clearly recognisable, in the centre, third row from the back

Chapter 7

St. Bernard's in the 1970s

HISTORICAL CONTEXT

1970   The Beatles split up

1971   Britain adopts decimal currency

1972   'Black September' Terrorist Group attack the Munich
        Olympics. Eleven Israeli athletes and officials killed

1973   Britain joins the European Economic Community

1974   Turkey invades Cyprus

1975   Death of Spanish dictator, Franco

1976   Concorde makes its first commercial flight

1977   Silver Jubilee of Queen Elizabeth II
        Elvis Presley dies

1978   First test-tube baby born in Britain

1979   Margaret Thatcher becomes first woman Prime
        Minister of Britain

~ 1970-1979 ~

St. Bernard's during the 1970s

In 1970, St. Bernard's celebrated its Diamond Jubilee and also saw the retirement of three of its long-established teachers, Mrs. Spary, Mrs. Greaves and Mrs. Lewis.

Miss O'Shaughnessy had been appointed headmistress in September 1969, with Sister Mary Stephen as her deputy. There were 700 students, nearly 80 of them in the sixth form. One of the sixth form, 'A' level English student **Teresa Fiore**, was successful in having three of her poems published in the *Book of 20th Century Poets*.

The school began a fundraising drive for a building fund for the new Jubilee building. A mammoth raffle was held, and a special Jubilee meeting of the Old Girl's Association attracted over 300 ex-students.

In May 1971, a special Diamond Jubilee Mass was held, and the fund-raising had obviously been successful as, in July 1972, the new building was officially opened. It was to be the new sixth form wing, now the north corridor.

In October 1972, Sister Marie Mildred celebrated her jubilee and in August 1974 the community were able to purchase Hyning Hall.

Miss O'Shaughnessy retired in 1976 and Sister Mary Stephen became headmistress, remaining in her post until 1983.

Memories of the 1970s

Valerie Wroe (née Huntington) attended St. Bernard's until 1974:

"Technology was advancing rapidly, and we found ourselves at St. Bernard's at the start of the computer age.

"As sixth formers, we were introduced to the first pocket calculator. It was about 9 inches long and 4 inches wide, ran out of batteries in a flash, but could add, subtract, multiply *and* divide!

"I don't know how much it cost, but I remember investing £25 in something similar the following year. Within a few years tiny versions were being given away on key rings.

"Our new and exciting maths teacher took us on a trip to see a computer. It had a brain about the size of a pea, and took up a whole room. Our teacher's name was Mr. Hind, and he had not long graduated from Cambridge. He taught us to throw away the rule-book and think outside the box. His lessons always seemed to end up as group discussions on some obscure point of maths.

"Sixteen years later, as a parent, I found myself at the first summer school for gifted children. As introductions were being made, my attention was on the man lying flat out in the corner. 'And the man asleep on the floor is Jim Hind, our maths and astronomy tutor'. At this point I knew my children would have a fantastic week.

"After the general introductions, I went up to say hello and, with a double take, his first words were, 'I used to teach you – St. Bernard's – Valerie Huntington.' They say teachers remember the good students and the bad ones. I wonder which I was?"

~~~~~~~~~~

SUZANNE PHILLIPS (née D'EATH) attended St. Bernard's from 1971-79 and is now an English teacher at the school:

"They say that school days are the best days of your life. However, when you're there this maxim doesn't always ring true. Nevertheless, with the passage of time, I now look back on my days at St. Bernard's as a time of development and growth, where I was nurtured and encouraged to find my true potential. Furthermore, I was lucky enough to attend when the nuns were still resident, so the school took on a homely, caring atmosphere that spilled over to surround and protect us girls.

"However, my most enduring memories are not of school work or exams, although I must admit that even now, when I find myself returned in the reversed role of teacher rather than pupil, I cannot descend the wooden staircase without remembering the fear and trepidation of waiting there in line, cramming last minute revision notes, before being herded into the hall to sit dreaded examinations.

"But for me, school was about the friendships that still endure today and those special teachers who inspired me to work – either out of fear or love. From the extremely strict Mrs. Miller, she of the twisted hair plaits, tweed skirts and sensible brogue shoes, who mercilessly drummed Latin verbs into us, yet inspired my love of ancient history, to Mrs. Short, the art teacher who rejoiced in creativity and revelled in artistic freedom, seeing 'art' where possibly there was very little – well in my case anyway. The list is endless:

"Miss O'Shaughnessy, headmistress, who resembled the 'dark crusader' in her black, bat-winged gown; Mrs. Bruce, the soft spoken English teacher; Mr. Ballard, the French teacher who eventually became headmaster; Miss O'Riordan, Maths demon; Mr. Garrard, physics teacher whose life we made a misery – many apologies; Sister Mary Ted, a nun with a true vocation, who was too saintly and trusting to be teaching the likes of us; Miss Blelloc who drilled us through the complicated steps of ballroom dancing before it became cool – and so the list continues.

"Needless to say, these people all had a special role in making me the person I am today. However, my days at St. Bernard's were also about growing up; bridging the gap between teenager and adult. So, throughout this metamorphosis, it is the friends that grew alongside me, and our escapades that endure in my memory and, believe me, the escapades seemed endless – from the greasing of door-handles to prevent teachers entering the class room, to the displaying of three foot 'Colditz' banners in the windows of the M.F.L. room overlooking Milton Road (a prank that Mr. Ballard did not find amusing) and all the other harmless japes that brightened up our days.

"Being at an all girls' school, I cannot end without mentioning boys and our fascination for the opposite sex – even today, when I am on gate duty and I see the spotty, gangling youths converging like magnets onto the school, I am reminded of the boyfriends who would come and collect us, and how we would peer out of the windows to see who was lurking around to meet whom. In particular I remember one such day, when lessons at the end of the day were disrupted by the sound of sirens as the fire brigade came screeching to a halt outside the school. Needless to say, we all ran to look out of the window, only to see my best friend's (Jane Harvey) latest boyfriend jumping around distraught, as his flashy new sports car erupted in a blaze of flames and smoke – it had mysteriously caught fire whilst he was parked (or should I say posing) outside. Luckily he escaped injury – although the same couldn't be said for his car –

and was ushered into the school by a huddle of concerned nuns, who offered him countless cups of tea to help drown his sorrows.

"However, I digress. But as anyone who has gone to St. Bernard's will know, it was, and still is, a special place that continues to endure and as such, I am proud to have been part of its history."

~~~~~~~~~~~~

LINDA KENTON (née ROTHMAN) remembers vividly a school trip to Greece in 1970:

"Although I found it hard at times, I remember having some really good times (even though I'm sure the teachers might not agree with me). I think we were definitely the rebellious class of the year. There were two grammar classes and two secondary classes per year. We were divided up as classes 1, 2, 3 and 4. Class 1 was the top half of the alphabet in the grammar stream, and class 2 was the second half of the alphabet. I'm not sure how the other two classes were formed, but I imagine it was the same way. I was in class 2. We always seemed to be getting into trouble far more than class 1 (but I'm sure we had more fun).

"Although I meet up with quite a lot of girls from my class at least once a year (about twenty of us) and we reminisce about loads of things, the one memory that sticks out for me is our trip to Athens. Quite adventurous, don't you think, to take a group of fifteen and sixteen-year-old girls to Athens? We were accompanied by Mrs. Miller, her husband and her son. We went on the train as far as Venice. Then we got on a ship that took us through the Corinth Canal. Sounds wonderful, but when we got on board the ship in Venice the cabins we were allocated were hot and smelly and down with the crew. In fact, we were so disgusted that we all decided to sleep on deck for the night. And that is exactly what we did. At least we were close by for the wonderful spectacle of sailing through the Corinth. Our holiday in Athens was good and we had a wonderful time. On our return journey, I celebrated my sixteenth birthday on board and was presented with a birthday cake by the crew. I even made the *Evening Echo* on our return."

~~~~~~~~~~~~

St. Bernard's trip to Greece in 1970, led by Mrs. Miller,
taken on the hills overlooking the Acropolis

Recapturing the glories of Greece. Some girls dancing at the Acropolis
(apologies for the poor quality image)

The exhausting train journey to Venice. Do you recognise anyone?

KIM RADFORD also remembers her time at the school:

"I started at St. Bernard's in 1970 – the Diamond Jubilee year – and left in 1977. Arriving on day one, we received a friendly welcome and we were all proud to be wearing our new uniforms – I still have the blazer, which I also wore on my last day in the sixth form. I have the straw boater too. The uniform was changed at the end of my first year, to a blue pinafore and blue and white checked blouse, with no tie, and a new cap style hat replaced the beret.

"We navigated around the building with reference to the different stairs – the stone, the wooden, the marble, the open-plan – and only got lost on a few occasions at the beginning. I recall the whole form trying to find the needlework room right up in the roof over the hall, next to the senior library. It was last lesson on a Friday afternoon at the end of our first week and then, when we finally found the room, we got told off for being late. We made a lot of creaking noise on those wooden stairs, too.

"Particular events, among many, that stick in my mind are: Mrs. Fry stopping a biology lesson so we could all watch the fire brigade rescue a cat which was stuck in a tree outside the laboratory window, in Canewdon Road, and also watching the results of the October 1974 General Election, sitting in our classroom (which was the only one with a television in it) with Sister Mary Stephen."

~~~~~~~~~~

St Bernard's is renowned for its plays. In 1972, the school staged a performance of the *Pirates of Penzance*. Here, **LESLEY HICKSON** has very clear memories of this event:

"Some of you may recognise yourselves in this photo of *The Pirates of Penzance* as well as your fellow pirates, beautiful maidens or policemen who clearly look as if 'a policeman's lot is not a happy one'. Sporting those moustaches, I'm not surprised. On seeing it, maybe the hilarious words of the songs and the wit of the dialogue will come back to you, especially those formulated in a kind of Victorian rap.

'They have no legal claim
'No shadow of a shame
'Will fall upon thy name'

"One song will trigger another and, if that does not work, just try the answer to most things, which is Google, and you will find the whole script and even a performance or two on YouTube. If you are still trying to come to terms with the Internet, having, like Frederick's nurse-maid, not only hit 47 years but passed it by some years back, then there is always the advice of the first lines:

'Pour o pour the pirate sherry,

Fill o fill the pirate glass.'

"Once you have taken off and remembered the pirate song, the poor wandering one, the song of the Modern Major General, there will be no stopping you. Remember to have a bit of consideration for others around who may not be so enthusiastic even if you sing in the spirit of the policemen:

'with cat-like tread, upon our prey we steal.

In silence dread, our cautious way we feel.

No sound at all, we never speak a word

A fly's footfall would be distinctly heard'

"Once I got the words up on screen, it all came back, but I was soon asked 'Are you going to sing the whole thing?' So sing alone or organise a *Pirates of Penzance* party, which reminds me that there is a karaoke version.

"Like the performances on YouTube, none of this is as much fun as those months in 1972 filled with rehearsals, the planning and painting of the scenery, which was only revealed in all its glory at the dress rehearsal, and the making of the costumes due to the hard work of Mrs. Stanmore, who was the relatively new music teacher on the staff, and Mrs. Lewis, who was of course an institution, having taught generations of pupils to at least thread a needle and at most make their own clothes.

"In the lead up to the night, I was reminded that the policemen were asked to perform at assembly to increase the sales of tickets and as a taster that it would be an amusing evening for performers and audience alike.

"Many years have passed since then and whether you have used some of the songs as party pieces, hummed them whilst cleaning the house or had forgotten them totally, I hope this photo will bring back memories of the fun of performing on stage for which St. Bernard's is and will hopefully always be renowned.

"I would like to thank both the pirate king (who promised us: 'I'll be true to the song I sing') and a daughter of the modern major general for their memories of March 1972."

The cast of the Pirates of Penzance in March 1972. The beautiful stage in the old school hall will be remembered fondly by former students

~~~~~~~~~~~

CHRIS WALLEN remembers the 'Baker Boy' hats and the pinafores that went all shiny and baggy. She remembers the nuns' washing on the line outside, and Mrs. Miller climbing out of her son's bubble car every morning.

~~~~~~~~~~~

TINA-MARIE SHAW (née BATTEN) also remembers starting at the school:

"It was the first year of the 'new block' (the bit over the top of the dining hall) and the first intake of that horrific uniform with the silly 'Princess Anne' hat and horrid tunic. By the third year, we had swapped the tunic for skirts, and the hats were never seen again."

~~~~~~~~~~~

MARIAN RUSTON (née Loughrey) attended the school in the 1970s, and is another 'old girl' who has since returned to work at the school:

"I remember being taken, in the summer term of 1975, for an interview with the Reverend Mother. I was a young child of ten years old, and it was a memory never to be forgotten. My mother and I sat in the entrance hall with tiled floor and fireplace, waiting to be called in. I don't have clear memories of what I was asked during the interview, just a vivid picture of the place that I was to be lucky enough to spend the next six years of my life in. My mother then took me to Horne's Outfitters to purchase the uniform; blue tunic with zip at the side, blue and white checked, 'Peter Pan' collar, nylon blouse, a very odd blazer that had no lapel and was made of the same material as the tunic, and blue shoes with white socks. I could feel the pride emanating from my dear mother, that I had been offered a place at such a prestigious school. I felt slightly nervous and wanted to do my very best to make her proud of me.

"My school days at St. Bernard's were happy ones, and I felt loved and nurtured there. The Sisters were kind and generous with their time and never failed to remind us of our service to God in life. I remember walking down a corridor whistling, and Sister Mary Joseph telling me that: 'If a lady whistled it made Our Mother cry.' These were words that I was to hear frequently. My favourite time of the day was Benediction before school in the wonderful chapel, which still remains pretty much as it was in the 1970s; such a peaceful time in the morning spent praying with the Sisters of the community. My time at St. Bernard's shaped my life and taught me many important life skills; we were taught to respect the convent, as it was the home of the Sisters and always to show reverence and love for others.

"I was not the most studious of pupils (as you can see from the report of my first year), but always tried my hardest. I failed the 11-plus examination, much to the disappointment of my dear mother and father (they would have dearly loved me to be in the grammar stream at St. Bernard's), and was, therefore, in the comprehensive stream of the school. At that time, the school was divided into forms: 1 and 2 being the grammar stream, and 3 and 4 being the comprehensive stream. I was Form 1:4. I did not come from a

Catholic feeder school, although I did know a few of my contemporaries through my parish churches of St. Gregory's, Thorpe Bay and St. George's, Shoeburyness. My best friend at school in the early days was Katy Maloney; we lived around the corner from each other and also attended Brownies together. Many a happy day was spent together, both at school and in each other's houses.

"I loved geography with Mrs. Mitchell; she was a very glamorous teacher, always wore wonderful high-heeled shoes, and looked very chic at all times. Mrs. Addicott was my R.E. teacher for some time and, although I'm sure I led her a merry dance, I loved her really. Mrs. Bailey and Mr. Ballard were my teachers for French and Mrs. Connelly for P.E. Sister Mary Joseph was not only my maths teacher, but a lovely form tutor as well. Mrs. Bruce taught me English, and I remember studying *The Merchant of Venice* with her; she was a very patient teacher and always afforded me extra time when I was struggling. I had typing and shorthand lessons with Mrs. Hooker; she had the longest, red-painted nails I had ever seen and, if my fingers were not on the home keys, she would elegantly place them in the correct position using her long nails.

"Sister Mary Stephen got to know me quite well as I was often seated outside her office on the wooden bench, waiting for a telling off for one thing or another (usually for sneaking off the school premises at lunch time to nip down to the Cliffs Pavilion for a sneaky cigarette; oh the shame). However, Sister Mary Stephen, although strict, was always fair, and it didn't take me long to confess to my wrong-doings and accept whatever punishment she felt fit for the crime.

"During my time at St. Bernard's, I remember being involved in some fundraising, for Sister Mary Joseph to take the sick children of the local parishes on a Diocesan trip in the 'Jumbulance'; much fun was had during this time, and lots of funds were raised in all manner of ways. She was truly an inspiration. I remember Sister Mary Vincent making wooden calendars to sell; she had an ingenious tool that burnt an etching in the balsa wood, and when varnished it looked beautiful.

"The most memorable school play was a production of *Oliver* that we performed (I was in the choir; I was neither a natural musician, nor a performer). Mr. Ballard played the part of Fagin; it was the most amazing production, and I have fond memories of the performance. I can still remember all the words to the songs.

1977 saw the Queen's Silver Jubilee, and much excitement was felt for such a regal occasion; I feel sure that we had a day off school to mark the occasion. Street parties were held all over the country; what a lovely, happy memory. Each child was presented with a mug and a commemorative coin to mark the occasion, and I remember our particular street party went on until the wee hours of the morning and united everyone in the neighbourhood.

After completing one year of sixth form, I left St Bernard's to take up employment. I once again found myself waiting to be interviewed at St. Bernard's twenty-four years later, in 1999, for a job interview; it felt very odd to be shown round in areas that were out of bounds as a pupil. I remember having the feeling of 'coming home', and many of the areas had not changed one bit. I still remain there today, and feel privileged that I have had the opportunity to enjoy once again the ethos and values of the school and to be involved with its growth and evolution. My two daughters have also since been educated in the school and their time there has been happy and fulfilling."

~~~~~~~~~~~

ST. BERNARD'S CONVENT HIGH SCHOOL
WESTCLIFF-ON-SEA, ESSEX.

Name _Marian Loughrey_   No. in form _31_

Form _I4._   Times absent _—_

Term _Autumn_   Times late _✓_

Next term begins _7ᵗʰ Jan._ ends _9ᵗʰ April . 1976._

SUBJECT	Attain-ment	Effort	REMARKS
Religious Knowledge			Marian has worked quite well and her written work is quite good. She could concentrate more in class. M.L.
English	C		Marian appeared to settle down well but lately her work has not been up to standard.
Mathematics	C		Improving — but Marian needs to work very hard at this subject. She is too slow at settling down to work. S.M.J
P.E.			Gymnastics Dance — Marion finds it difficult to work sensibly and with co-operation; much improved. E.D.
Science	B		Marian has made some progress but she must try to concentrate more.
Art			If Marion thought about her own work she could do well. M.
French	B-		Marion has produced some good work but she must concentrate all the time. SB.
History			She works satisfactorily
Geography	C		Written work needs more effort, orally works well with enthusiasm.
Needlework	B-		Good PD

Now that Marian has settled down in her new school she should be able to improve her general standard of work by giving her full attention during lessons next term.

Form Mistress _Sr. Mary Joseph OC_

Headmistress _AO Loughnessy_

Marian Ruston, one of the editors, has bravely provided
her first school report from St. Bernard's

The following memories were found in a newsletter from the end of 1978. It was decided that, instead of the head teacher writing an end-of-year report, she would ask staff and students to write their own memories of the school. Sadly, the author is unknown.

"Having reached the grand old age of eighteen, I can afford to sit back in my rocking-chair and reflect on the past seven years – the years I spent as a pupil of St. Bernard's. It may sound 'corny', but I must say that St. Bernard's has played an important part in my life – after all, I did spend practically half my life within her walls. You could even say that from the first trembling, panic-stricken moments way back in 1971 to the last emotional week only a month ago, the convent filled my every waking moment – the staff give you so much homework that there's no time for anything else.

"At the age of eleven and the grand height of 3ft 6ins, I found St. Bernard's a vast, towering emporium, soon to be named 'Colditz' in the heart of every miserable first year. But everything mellows with time, and by the time I and my friends of 1.2 reached our last days in upper sixth, St. Bernard's had become less of a prison and more of a home. In fact, I think every pupil would agree that there is something special about the convent – a warmth provided by those strange figures in black and white floating around – the nuns.

"To the surprise of many non-St. Bernardites, I didn't spend 90 per cent of the last seven years on my knees; my school years were pretty much like anybody else's – after all, we used to hide in the cupboards during history lessons and once tried to tape a particularly irate late teacher during one of our favourite lessons – and I also remember our sister class greasing the door handle and tying the chalk to a length of thread so that it mysteriously moved every time the poor maligned teacher reached forth her hand.

"Those seven years consisted of lessons, laughter and friendship, and that last quality is perhaps the main factor of everybody's school life and one of the reasons we all found it so hard to leave. The friends and enemies of seven years floated before the eyes through a haze of tears and the debris of the sixth form sherry party for the staff.

"I think that I really came to enjoy my time at St. Bernard's once I reached the sixth form, once I was there voluntarily, not being dragged to school by the scruff of the neck every morning; but I wouldn't say that I'd absolutely hated the previous five years. Games lessons and occasional holidays punctuated the grim horror of seven lessons a day, five days a week. Life, even at the convent, wasn't always a bed of roses but the warmth I experienced on my first day, in the person of 'Sister V' as she will always be known to us all, was present right up to the day I left.

"One of the special qualities of St. Bernard's was, and still is, the community spirit which extended beyond the 9-5 routine of the other secondary schools in the area. Outside school hours, staff and pupils were still members of the world-wide Bernardine family.

"We used to sing the school song every year at prize-giving, a custom which belonged to an era of straw boaters, gymslips and Latin grammars – an era I saw, but never took part in. My straw boater was never taken out of the cupboard. That famous, or infamous, song always made me want to laugh (rather embarrassing in front of massed parents and governors at prize-giving), and I think that even the staff and community would agree that some of the lines were unfortunate, although presumably well-intentioned, for example: 'A child of St Bernard's is known everywhere.' Yet another line: 'Sing we the house that we all love so dearly', sums up my memories of St. Bernard's as I sit here. No present pupil would agree, but I feel you have to leave in order to realise how much you miss it."

Chapter 8

St. Bernard's in the 1980s

HISTORICAL CONTEXT

1980   Mount St. Helens erupts in Washington State, U.S.A.

1981   Royal Wedding of Prince Charles and Lady Diana

1982   Argentina invades the Falkland Islands

1983   Margaret Thatcher wins her second General Election, this time by a landslide

1984   I.R.A. bomb attack at the hotel in Brighton in which Prime Minister, Margaret Thatcher, is staying

1985   Britain and the Irish Republic sign the Anglo-Irish Agreement

1986   28th January: the space shuttle 'Challenger' explodes, killing all on board

1987   16th October: a 'hurricane' sweeps across southern England, causing massive damage

1988   'Free Nelson Mandela' concert held at Wembley Stadium

1989   The Berlin Wall comes down

~ 1980-1989 ~

St. Bernard's during the 1980s

In 1980, St. Bernard's celebrated the 1,500th anniversary of the birth of St. Benedict with a special edition of the school magazine and the creation of a tapestry quoting St. Benedict, 'Prefer nothing to the love of Christ,' made by Mrs. Connolly's husband. This was displayed in the reception area until 1995. Pupils at the school at this time were also given the opportunity to visit Rome on a school trip, which included an audience with the Pope.

In February 1982, it was announced that from September 1983 the Bernardine Community would withdraw from Westcliff, due to falling numbers, but there would be two new communities, in Slough and Hyning. Initially, this move was to be for a period of five years, and then it would be reviewed. In a letter to parents from Sister Mary Lucy, Mother Superior wrote about how the Community would still play a role in school life:

"The school, however, will continue to belong to the order, which will still maintain direction of it through the governing body, on which our Sisters will continue to serve and keep in close contact with the whole school community.

"At the end of the five year period, the position will be reviewed, and it is hoped that our numbers will allow us once again to form a third community."

Sister Mary Stephen resigned as head teacher as from 31st December 1982, and John Ballard was appointed head teacher from 1st January 1983.

1985 saw the 75th anniversary of St. Bernard's and, despite his efforts, Mr. Ballard was unable to get Cardinal Basil Hume to come to Westcliff to officiate Mass on this special occasion. A buffet was held in the school hall to celebrate the anniversary, and an outdoor end of year Mass was held.

In education, the National Curriculum for maths and science was introduced in 1989.

Sister Mary Stephen, John Ballard and Miss O'Shaughnessy, celebrating the school's
75th Anniversary in 1985. All had been head teachers at St. Bernard's

MEMORIES OF THE 1980s

JANE HARRIS (née DOWNEY) attended St Bernard's from 1976-83:

"I have many happy memories of my years at St. Bernard's and
even cried at the sixth form Leaving Mass in 1983. I was also lucky
enough to have been there whilst the Community was still active,
and I think we all benefited from their presence. I shall never forget Sister Hedwige, as the 'Knitting Nun', who was always knitting
woolly hats for us.

"In 1980, I was lucky enough to go on the school trip to Rome.
Aside from the skiing trips, for me, there had not been many opportunities to go on a school trip. So, in 1980, we all set off for a trip
to Rome and the southern part of Italy. We set off by coach from
Westcliff to Calais, and then picked up the overnight train from
Calais to Milan. Sister Mary Vincent was very concerned that some
of us may have been in the wrong part of the train when it split up
in Switzerland, and we were under strict instructions not to leave
our carriages. Unfortunately, upon our arrival in Milan, our courier
from the travel company discovered his mother was ill, and he had
to return home. This left us without a courier. Fortunately a mother, who was helping, spoke Italian. However, we managed to keep

to a basic itinerary, and Miss Fossey, who had organised the trip, managed very well to keep us organised, possibly the hardest part being to keep away the hoards of Italian boys that followed us everywhere. News seems to have spread very quickly that there was a party of English schoolgirls staying in the local hotel. The hotel was very basic, and we eventually got used to the cockroaches in the rooms, and yesterday's bread rolls.

"However, apart from the Italian boys, the main trip was to see the sights of Rome and visit the Vatican. I will never forget going to Mass, taken by Pope John Paul II, and being lucky enough to have an aisle seat, so that when he walked down the aisle, I was only feet away from him. We were also part of the Wednesday afternoon audience in St Peter's Square, where the Pope toured the Square in the 'Popemobile' and the school's name was read out to the assembled crowd. The rest of the trip consisted of visits to the Catacombs, the Basilica and finally, at the end of the week, a trip to Assisi and Pompeii.

"The trip home was completed with a very bumpy crossing back to Dover."

~~~~~~~~~~

Class 5J in 1981(photograph supplied by Jane Harris, née Downey)

JOHANNA WYLDE (née BAILLIE) remembers her time at the school:

"It was the year of 1987, and my first day at St. Bernard's. I remember we had to congregate in the hall, where I heard the first 'headmaster' speech from Mr. Ballard, sitting on the wooden chairs with a green metal frame.

"To be honest, I was in awe of the school. You could feel the history of the place as you walked around it. The nuns' quarters upstairs always had people talking about ghostly things they had heard.

"The major task after leaving junior school was trying to find your way around the new school, so I had my own landmarks:

"The chocolate button stairs;
"The red stairs;
"The sparkly stairs; and
"The wooden stairs

"My years at St. Bernard's were quite quiet really. The two things that stand out were the Gulf War, and the dispute concerning one of the teachers, which resulted in all the pupils going on strike. I didn't even know the teacher concerned at the time, but it seemed the done thing to follow everyone else and sit on the field. It even got into the local paper.

"Mrs. Mitchell was one of the loveliest teachers I encountered. She taught history with such a passion. It soon became apparent, from the first lesson, how much she loved the colour pink and on occasions would wear her favourite pale pink heels. Her handwriting was also very memorable and beautiful.

"Mrs. Carmichael taught me French, German and R.E. She would always walk into the classroom and say 'Bonjour' when it was a German lesson, and 'Guten Morgan' when it was French. I think she gave up saying anything when it was R.E.

"I thank St. Bernard's for giving me some great years of schooling, fond memories and some lifelong friends."

~~~~~~~~~~~~

Another 'old girl' is **JAQUI PATTERSON**, who attended the school from 1945 to 1956 and returned as a teacher from 1963-94:

"How is the illusive 'Bernardine Spirit' defined? Maybe it is by the commitment 'to prefer nothing to the love of Christ'; to lead with wisdom and with love; to inspire each person to reach one's full potential.

"Not only am I an 'old girl' of St. Bernard's, I also taught at the school for more than thirty years.

"On that painful day, as the Bernardine Community left Westcliff, their final entreaty to a small group of teachers gathered to bid a reluctant farewell was, 'You must keep the Bernardine Spirit alive here at Westcliff.'

"And that is precisely what the governors and staff, pupils and parents at St. Bernard's have endeavored to fulfil. That the Bernardine Spirit still permeates throughout the school is indisputable."

~~~~~~~~~~

SARAH ANNE COTGROVE has many memories, such as:

"Mr. McEwan getting locked in the computer cupboard, students protesting about using mice in science and throwing them out of the window into the street. I remember the brilliant trip to Moscow and Leningrad that Mrs. Voller took us on. I remember the older girls terrifying us with legends of old nuns who haunted the attic rooms, and daring each other to go up there alone.

"I also remember being genuinely inspired by Mrs. Cooper, the English teacher, who really helped and encouraged me in writing stories (I still do it today because of her … if I ever get published she'll get a cut).

"I remember the chocolate button stairs and the toilets that had a hole in the back where you could pass cigarettes through to each other. It really wasn't worth the wrath of Miss Donohoe if she caught you.

"Our uniform was also the cause of much rule-breaking. I remember kneeling on the floor in R.E. to check that our skirts were not too short, and being followed everywhere by teachers yelling: 'Tuck your shirt in.'

"A couple more things I remember are: doing cross country at St. Thomas More, where we all tried to catch a glimpse of our favourite Tommy More boy; the feeling of dread when your name was called out on the Tannoy system."

~~~~~~~~~~~

JEN WIGLEY-SNOW, who attended St. Bernard's from 1975 to 1982, has a particular memory of a pilgrimage to Rome in 1981:

"The group was supposed to have a private audience with Pope John Paul II, but unfortunately, he was too ill. However, they did manage to have a public audience with him instead."

~~~~~~~~~~~

ANDREW CAMPBELL joined St. Bernard's sixth form during 1981, which was the first year the school allowed boys to join the lower sixth:

"I can tell you it was quite a culture shock after having spent five years at the all-boys St. Thomas More School. We were made to feel very welcome in the school. I think many of the teachers had no experience of male pupils, so they probably related to us more as adults, even if we didn't always behave that way.

"Although limited in numbers, we soon made ourselves useful by helping Mr. Carter (caretaker) move various pianos about the school, plus covering the male roles in various productions."

~~~~~~~~~~~

A photograph of the first sixth form boys in 1981, supplied by Andrew Campbell

LAURA PANTER (née OLD) attended the school from 1987 to 1994, and has since returned as a biology teacher. She remembers snippets from her time as a student:

"An interview in the head's office; a first bus journey; a new form, a new uniform; the wooden stairs; the slope in the garden; drama in the drama studio; bend-zee-knees-and-swing-zee-arms;

"Hobb's Cross Farm; Flashdance at the talent show; Je suis un arbre dans la ville;

"Sandwiches, dinners or snacks; canis est in via; discos at St. Helens;

"The British Museum; 'Can you tell me where the Rosetta Stone is please'? 'you're sitting on it.'

"Making a clock from perspex in technology; washing up water fights in food tech;

"The red stairs; the Mary Poppins' view across the roof tops from the biology lab;

"A collective sense of humour; cake sales; running in P.E. knickers along the seafront;

"Eating boiled fish eyes for comic relief; the Latin trip to Sorrento; Guiseppe with the squeaky voice; the road to Herculaneum;

"Work experience; a student strike; the art room's nooks and crannies;

"The chocolate button stairs; the preserved specimens in the dem lab; George Harrison singing *Here comes the Sun*;

"Shine Jesus Shine; Mr. Castle's use of *Winnie the Pooh* to teach us respect for each other; P.S.E. days and *The Dead Poets Society*;

"Relaxing to music in the art room while a plaster of Paris mask dries on my face;

"Gandhi; *Caravan of Love* by the House Martins;

"The Stone Stairs; Desmond Tutu; the little sixth form lab;

"Digging a pond for an ecology garden; the final advent service in the Baptist Church;

"The biology field trip; the stage; the passion play; rag week; the open-air feast day Masses;

"Breaking the microphone; leavers' assemblies; the sunlight streaming through the tall windows of the hall;

"The clip-clopping of heels on parquet floors as invigilators monitored exam candidates;

"Results day."

A group of Year 7 pupils from 1983. Unfortunately we have no information about them. Do you recognise anyone?

Chapter 9

St. Bernard's in the 1990s

HISTORICAL CONTEXT

1990	Margaret Thatcher forced to resign as Prime Minister. She is replaced by John Major
1991	The Gulf War begins
1992	Betty Boothroyd elected as Speaker of the House of Commons. She is the first woman to hold this role
1993	A terrorist bomb explodes under the World Trade Centre in New York
1994	Nelson Mandela becomes South Africa's first black President
1995	Head teacher Philip Lawrence murdered outside his school in London
1996	Dunblane Massacre in a Scottish school
1997	31st August: Princess Diana dies in a car crash; Mother Teresa dies a few days later on 5th September
1998	Omagh bombing in Northern Ireland
1999	People around the world celebrate the new millennium on New Year's Eve

~ 1990-1999 ~

St. Bernard's during the 1990s

On 31st August 1990, the Bernardine Sisters formally handed over control of the school to the Diocese of Brentwood. The name of the school changed from 'St. Bernard's Convent High School for Girls' to 'St. Bernard's High School'.

Also in 1990, Mr. Ballard had to announce to the governors that the Secretary of State had decided not to support the proposed amalgamation of St. Bernard's and St. Thomas More High Schools. The possible amalgamation had had a detrimental impact on St. Bernard's over the previous few years, as investment in the buildings seemed unnecessary if the school was to move to the St. Thomas More site within the next three years. However, once the proposed amalgamation had been rejected, the governors were anxious to reactivate plans for the development of the St. Bernard's building, and that every attempt should be made to make up for lost time. Local management of schools came into force in 1990 and, in April 1991, St. Bernard's received their delegated budget. The full responsibility for the school's budget was now in the hands of the governors.

During 1991, the school buildings were completely renovated externally, with new roofs on most of the buildings. All wooden framed windows were replaced with double glazed P.V.C. frame windows and the stonework repaired.

A new shower block and changing rooms were added to the south wing in 1992, and these were extended to include a multi-gym in 1993.

The status of the school changed in 1994, when St. Bernard's became a grant-maintained school. This involved the development of a new finance and premises department, with Mr. Bill Sanders as its first premises manager.

In 1995, Mr. Ballard retired following a twenty-five-year career at the school; first as head of languages, then as deputy head teacher and finally as head teacher from 1983. Mr. Ballard's request to have the chapel bell as his leaving present was honored and the Feast Day Mass in July was treated as a special goodbye, with a Mass conducted on the playground by four local priests. Afterwards, a lunch was given for guests and staff, and students had a picnic lunch and games in the grounds.

Miss Squirrell was appointed head teacher from September 1995. In 1996, a survey of the buildings was conducted, and a plan to systematically upgrade the facilities was agreed. A year later, plans were drawn up for a multi-purpose sports hall to be built.

In 1998, as part of Miss Squirrell's 'ten-year school development plan', the science department underwent complete modernisation. Six new science laboratories were built using a new 'pod' layout. In 1999, the technology department was also brought up to date; three classrooms in the west wing were stripped out and rebuilt to make two large workshops and a technician's room.

MEMORIES OF THE 1990S

BRYONY TAYLOR (née Hall), was deputy head girl in 1995:

"Everyone says they remember where they were when J.F.K. was assassinated. Well I can remember where I was when Margaret Thatcher resigned in November 1990. We were in a French lesson with Miss Ginnity, and Miss Donohoe burst into the classroom and announced 'Mrs. Thatcher has resigned'. We all cheered. I assume Miss Donohoe made her way round the other classrooms as well. She must have heard the news on the radio.

"The school was evacuated once for a bomb scare. This was at the height of paranoia about I.R.A. attacks. It was actually just a prank call. It was very disconcerting though: coming back from P.E. down at Westcliff Leisure Centre and seeing the whole school sitting cross-legged on the playground.

"I was in a few school productions: *The Sorcerer*, directed by Mrs. Bell (née Sleightholme); *Guys and Dolls*, directed by Mr. Hardingham, and *Twelfth Night*, which we did in the style of *Pulp Fiction*, which had just come out, also directed by Jerry Hardingham.

"In about 1993, an *It's a Knockout* was organised by Mr. Elmes. It culminated in a very daring run by a girl called Kim O'Neill to pour a bucket of water over Miss Donohoe, who was merely watching. She was not impressed, but Kim went down as a legend for years amongst the girls (editors' note: Miss Donohoe actually denies this happening).

"For some reason, all the P.E. teachers in the early 1990s wore these bizarre ankle socks with bobbles attached to the heel part of the sock. They became a P.E. department trade mark.

"We used to play hockey at the Tommy More field, which we dubbed 'Siberia' because of how freezing it always was.

"Badminton was great fun because we played in the hall. There was a statue of Jesus on the wall with his arms outstretched: far too tempting to a group of girls playing badminton. The aim of the game was to get a shuttlecock to land on one of Jesus' hands. It was always exciting to spot a shuttlecock there in assembly, realising that Mr. Sanders, the caretaker, hadn't noticed it yet."

~~~~~~~~~~

LIZ HOLLAND (née ALEXANDER) was a pupil from 1992-97:

"I was a pupil of St. Bernard's from 1992 to 1997, and Jon had attended St. Thomas More during this time. Beginning the sixth form in 1997, we were in the same form together and shared the same classes, where we became good friends. After a short while, we began seeing each other and continued to do so throughout the remainder of the sixth form until leaving in 1999, by which time we were engaged. We were married in 2003, and in 2007 our first child, Joseph, was born. Our little girl, Isabel, was born in 2009. We can thank the tradition of boys from St. Thomas More attending the sixth form at St. Bernard's for us having met, without which we may never have crossed paths. It was the caring family atmosphere that the school provided, which gave us the grounding for our relationship and our life together.

"During our time in the sixth form, we took part in many of the traditional activities, including: rag week; the talent show, when the boys were sold off in a slave auction (with Jack selling for an extremely high bid to a teacher and Jon going for a few pence); and the passion play, with Jason's brave performance, wearing a loin cloth in front of a hall full of girls. Another great memory was an R.E. trip to St. John the Baptist Monastery in Tiptree, with Mr. Castle driving the minibus. This was at the height of the 1998 World Cup, and as we travelled along the A12, we held up signs to passing motorists, encouraging them to honk in support of England in their game against Argentina. Those who didn't honk got an alternative sign that Jon and Jack had made. It's amazing that Mr. Castle managed to keep his mind on the road and that we didn't instigate any road-rage incidents.

"All in all, we had a great time at St. Bernard's and feel grateful that we both decided to attend the same school. We still keep in contact with good friends we made during our time at the school, and it's nice to see the families of our friends growing too."

~~~~~~~~~~

Liz and Jon Holland with their children, Joseph and Isabel outside Our Lady of Lourdes Church, on the occasion of Isabel's baptism

Patricia Frost (née O'Neill) remembers:

"I was at the school from 1989 to 1994. There was a sixth form boy called Norman Aldridge, and I think he was going out with either Juliette Johnson or Dawn Jenkins, who were a couple of years above us. I envied them so much because they knew all the boys, but mainly because they had the guts to wear red 'kickers' to school.

"I also remember the Italian dinner lady, Mrs. Dhillioni. She was lovely; she used to wipe the tables clean and wave her hand in the air for you to come and sit down, as she said: 'Move along girls.'

"Also, I remember when little James Bulger was snatched and murdered in 1993. We had to pray for the Bulger family every morning in registration, as our form teacher, Mrs. Goestchel, also had a little boy the same age as him.

"We also had another great supply teacher, Mr. Frisby, who was an old man but so funny … me and Angie loved him, he told such funny stories and sometimes wore a funny hat too.

"Mrs. Mitchell was another favourite of mine … the way she used to teeter along the library corridor in her high heels, lugging her briefcase with her. Then she'd throw it on the desk but, because she was so small, we would have to wait for her to climb on the stool, and she'd say: 'Morning ladies,' before we could see her. I remember, my sister and I were the only ones who travelled to school on the Tilbury train line, and once, when there was a terrible storm, we didn't arrive at school until lunchtime. Mrs. Patterson ushered us straight into the canteen for some 'hot soup', and said we could go home straight after dinner so we wouldn't be late. We thought it was great, so sometimes we were late even when the trains were fine. I remember being forty minutes late for one of my G.C.S.E.'s because of the trains. It was in the days before mobile phones. I tried so hard to come into the hall quietly, but the doors were so creaky.

"Then there was the head-of-year room – the place we had to go to during lunch and break if we had been naughty. I remember standing out there once with Syrita Nolan, who had been put on report for having half her hair short and the other side in a bob (permed and scrunched, of course).

"I can't remember what I had done wrong on that particular occasion – not that I was naughty!

"I remember a school disco once, after school. I had to leave early to catch the train, and Mr. Ballard wouldn't let me go, so he ended up driving me about twenty-five miles home. I also remember those socks the P.E. teachers wore – I think Mrs. Werry was the trendsetter for those.

"Standing in the toilets at lunch time, forever 'drying' our hands, just so we could stay in the warm when it was cold.

"I remember we used to dare each other to run up and down the 'staff stairs' from the ground floor, by what used to be the language corridor, up to the heads-of-year room, without being caught."

~~~~~~~~~~

RUTH BURKE (née CLAYDON) recalls the journeys to and from the school:

"I caught the train from Basildon to Westcliff. A big group of us used to all travel together. The train left Basildon at 8.02am, and I used to travel with Liz and Donna and some others. There were also quite a lot of boys from St. Thomas More.

"The best thing about travelling on the train was that we were often late, but were never told off. We also got to leave early if there was snow. We had a massive snowball fight at Westcliff Station on one particular occasion.

"Whenever I was sent home ill, the secretary used to say: 'Sit in the third class carriage, with the window open, next to a lady.' I never knew what she meant by 'third class'. Did it exist in 1996?

"The trains were 'slam-door' trains, and we used to delay the train by leaving the door open, whilst everyone else ran over the footbridge to get the train home.

"Other memories are of breaktime, spent hiding in the fire escape out of the rain, and the open-air whole school Masses at the end of the year.

"When we got into the sixth form, Miss Hayes was lovely to us, and we felt like proper grown-ups. Jack Whitaker was elected head boy as all the first years had a crush on him. The rules were quickly changed to prevent this happening again: now you have to be a pupil for more than two years before you can be elected."

~~~~~~~~~~

Zoe Richards recollects, amongst other things, the journeys from Canvey:

"I lived on Canvey and used to get the contract bus to school – not that it arrived on time. I remember one time it snowed really badly and the bus company wanted to take us home (it had taken until 9am to reach the Hadleigh roundabout), but Miss Squirrell made them continue driving us in. I can't remember what time we arrived, but not that long after, she made them take us home again.

"My favourite teachers were Miss Early and Miss Hayes. Mr. Elmes was cool too … he came to Peru with some of us.

"I was made prefect and enjoyed it too. Our Leavers' Assembly made most of the year cry, as they played R.E.M.'s *Everybody Hurts*. It can still make me teary when I hear it now."

~~~~~~~~~~

Michelle Kelly (née Howes) attended the school from 1995 to 2002:

"We used to scare ourselves silly with stories of the nuns. We thought that the old lift by the office was haunted, and we would sit in the doorways between the toilets and the P.E. showers, and tell ghost stories.

"In year 9, my friends and I used to hide round the corner at the sink to try to get Mrs. Ronan to lock us in our form room. One day she did, and we were all desperate for the loo. We never did it again, plus we all got a telling off when Mrs. Ronan came back."

~~~~~~~~~~

Katy Walford says that the things which stick in her mind are:

"How rolling your skirt up at least three times was mandatory, even though it was pleated and made you look like you either had a frill on the end of your jumper or a lampshade stuck around your waist;

"How the girls on the Canvey contract bus were always getting into bother for being far too loud;

"How everyone, at one point or another, threatened to kidnap Mr. Sheehan's penguin toy;

"Rag week, the annual passion play, and the whole-school Masses which would go on for about three hours, which was great as it normally meant missing double science or something;

"The year the whole school fancied a lad in the sixth form and voted him head boy;

"The hangovers every Wednesday and Thursday after the entire sixth form had been to either Chameleon or T.O.T.S. the night before!"

~~~~~~~~~~~

LIBBY GRACIE remembers specifically an event that still takes place today in the season of advent:

"The lighting of the advent candle, on a Friday night, by the tree in the reception area, was very warming. Hundreds of girls rushing to get home after a long hard week, and yet a handful of girls stayi-ing back for a short prayer and a carol.

"I also remember the chapel, and Mr. Castle's christening re-enactment, which I think he did with every class, every year.

"My favourite personal memory was being asked by Miss Donohoe to present a gift to a priest in front of everyone at the end of our Leavers' Mass. He decided to plant a kiss on my cheek … and I was not expecting that. My face was a picture, apparently. Well, its not everyday you get kissed by a priest. It tickled Miss Donohoe, and she gave me a certificate at the end of school for beng the 'best presenter of gifts to priests'."

~~~~~~~~~~~

It seems rag week is an event that sticks in many ex-students' mem-ories. It is a chance for the new head student team to organise a week of events to raise money for charity. It usually includes a 'teacher talent show' which is a big hit with the students. NAZIA NAAZ NABI states:

"I remember one rag week, when Mr. Harvey dressed as a woman with a blonde wig, and Mr. Elmes, Mr. Clarke and Mr. Staines all sang *Uptown Girl.*"

~~~~~~~~~~~

Mr. Harvey, deputy head teacher, being 'soaked' during rag week, 1993

The staff panto in 1993, showing Mr. Elmes and Mr. Harvey in 'drag'

During this decade, the first students were given the opportunity to take part in the Duke of Edinburgh Award Scheme. **MIKE ELMES** joined the school in 1990 and explains how the scheme is implemented within St. Bernard's:

"Having joined St. Bernard's in 1990, a senior teacher quickly spotted the potential of introducing the scheme to our students. Her name was Helen Crooks and she approached me about helping with the scheme, which I did in the following year, 1991. Helen also introduced activity weekends, which I took over upon Miss Crooks' appointment as deputy head at another school. The award went from strength to strength, but the expedition section was outsourced to an activity organisation until 1995, when I persuaded other members of staff to make up a team to run expeditions internally.

"Approximately 2,000 students have participated in the award so far, with over 1,200 completing bronze, silver and gold.

"In that time, we have also had many staff give of their free time on countless weekends through the years. At least four of the present staff are volunteers who have worked with me for ten years. Several others are approaching that figure. It is also gratifying that new staff members have joined the team. Also helping as volunteers are members of the sixth form. Their help is invaluable.

"Bronze participants meet every Thursday between 4.00pm and 6.00pm to complete their award and to train for the expedition phase. Silver and gold groups meet periodically to plan their expeditions. Destinations include: Danbury in Essex; the South Downs in Sussex; the Yorkshire Dales and the Cumbrian Lakes.

"There have also been gold expeditions to India and Peru as part of a month's trekking, and voluntary service through the World Challenge organisation. It is very much hoped that a centenary expedition to some far-flung destination will take place.

"The culmination of their dedication to the award, after completing the gold, is a trip to meet H.R.H. the Duke of Edinburgh at St. James' Palace, Buckingham Palace or Windsor Castle."

Mr Elmes is dedicated to the Duke of Edinburgh's Award and the School is extremely grateful to him for mentoring so many youngsters through the scheme.

~~~~~~~~~~

A group of girls taking part in the Silver Duke of Edinburgh expedition, in 2009.
The number of girls participating continues to grow

Activity weekends were introduced in 1990, primarily for students of years 7 and 8. These continued to run until 2007.

The weekends introduced students to the concept of outdoor learning, through activities such as orienteering, climbing, scrambling, canoeing, assault courses, night hikes and evening games.

It is very much hoped that these weekends can be reintroduced in the near future, as so many students gained so much in confidence through participating in the activities, and learnt very important life skills along the way.

Two very successful expeditions were led by Mr. Elmes, in 1998 to India, and in 2000 to Peru. The duration of the trips was four weeks during the summer holidays, and each trip consisted of up to twenty Year 11 and sixth form students, along with three members of staff.

The aim was to trek both the Himalayas and the Andes, reaching heights of 15,600 feet and 21,300 feet respectively. The treks through the mountain passes lasted ten days. The rest of the time was spent on community service at a Dali Lama school in Minali, Himashel Pradesh, northern India, where students helped decorate classrooms, teach, build new steps and reroute a stream. Also enjoyed were cultural visits, including the Taj Mahal, which was a splendid sight.

The Peruvian experience took place in northern Peru, and the community service took place in a favella, organised by the charity Plan International. Here again, students worked with the local school.

It is hoped that we can celebrate our centenary by organising another expedition for 2010-11.

A group photograph of the World Challenge group in Peru in 2000.
The trip lasted four weeks

Chapter 10

St. Bernard's in the New Millennium

HISTORICAL CONTEXT

2000	Catherine Hartle becomes the first British woman to reach the South Pole overland
2001	The World Trade Centre in New York is destroyed
2002	The Queen Mother dies, aged 101
2003	The second Gulf War
2004	26th December: Asian tsunami kills more than 200,000 people from 23 countries
2005	Pope John Paul II dies; 7th July: terrorist attacks on London
2006	Former Iraqi President, Saddam Hussein, sentenced to death
2007	Bulgaria and Romania join the European Union
2008	Barack Obama is elected the U.S.A.'s first black President
2009	North Korea tests nuclear missiles, breaking test ban treaty

~ 2000-2009 ~

St. Bernard's in the New Millennium

The school celebrated the arrival of the new millennium with a historical pageant that celebrated, in word, costume and song, the previous 1,000 years of British history. The doomsday 'Millennium Bug', that so many had predicted, failed to materialise and (perhaps to the secret disappointment of some staff) the computers did not die.

Unfortunately, this decade of St. Bernard's century, although a successful one for the school, has been affected by national and international crises. The terrorist attacks on the World Trade Centre in the United States had their own impact in the school, with many girls having family and business connections with the U.S.A. In 2005, the terrorist bombings in London brought the terrorist threat even closer to home, and many girls had to wait anxiously to hear news of parents, brothers, sisters and other relatives working in London that day.

On a happier note, the school went through an Ofsted inspection in October 2006 and achieved the category of 'Outstanding School'.

The site itself has continued to grow; this decade has seen the development of: new sporting facilities with the Bernardine Hall in 2001; the new arts building, with facilities for dance, drama, music and textiles in 2004; and, the very latest addition, in 2009, a new sixth-form study centre on the Milton Road playground.

Other achievements this decade have been: St. Bernard's girls' Year 8 football team winning the Coca-Cola Challenge; the chamber choir winning the Chas Waller Shield for the third time; and the school being ranked in the top 5 per cent best performing schools in the country.

In June 2000, St. Bernard's was identified by the *Daily Express* as one of the Top 50 schools in the country for assisting pupils to break out of the poverty trap and achieve top grades. In that year, St. Bernard's had more than 10 per cent of pupils on free school meals, yet 72 per cent of students gained five 'A-C' grades at G.C.S.E.

St. Bernard's has obviously changed significantly over the last 100 years. The most obvious sign of this is the dramatic increase in buildings from the original site. The Community of Bernardine Sisters is no longer present at Westcliff, but the homely nature of the school still makes itself felt, and this is something upon which visitors often comment. The presence of the religious community over so many years has obviously left an indelible mark.

Despite the many changes, however, one is struck again and again by what has stayed the same. The sense of fun and creativity of the students, the pleasure in the performing arts and sports, the commitment of so many members of staff over the years to the education of young people to the highest levels, and the real sense of community.

'The Head Teacher's Report' of 1966 is just as valid today as it was when it was written, forty years ago: 'The future is always shrouded in uncertainty, but what is certain is that St. Bernard's will continue to give the Christian education to which it is committed. Methods change, and we must be ready to change too. But our purpose remains unaltered: to prepare young women with complete and rounded personalities, who will play an active part in building a better world and devote themselves generously to the service of God and their fellow men.'

MEMORIES OF THE 2000s

PAULA DE BURGH attended St. Bernard's from 1998 to 2003. She remembers in particular the building of the sports hall:

"Whilst I attended St. Bernard's, the new sports hall was built. As you can imagine, there was great commotion as it was built. I personally arranged for a time capsule to be buried underneath the building. It contained such items as school uniform, badges and books. With the help of Mrs. Clancy, we found a time capsule in the form of a grey plastic pipe.

"Now I understand the significance of memorabilia and how this could be a historical find for future generations. However, I distinctly remember that, at the time, I came up with this plan in order to miss more P.E. lessons. Apologies, Mrs. Werry and Miss Purvis.

"Let us just say, most of my St. Bernard's life consisted of 'missing P.E.' plans – I also took part in the historical fashion show, made many trips abroad and knew P.E. dates so well that I scheduled in advance every dentist and doctors appointment."

~~~~~~~~~~~

KIM FORDHAM attended the school from 2000 to 2007 and remembers a history trip to the First World War battlefields in Ypres, Belgium, that she went on in Year 12.

"We were only a small history group, about five in total, and found it hard to hide our excitement at the proposed trip to Belgium. As every new detail of the trip was given to us, our excitement grew to new levels. I remember being particularly excited about visiting an actual trench and the town of Ypres itself.

"In the weeks leading up to the trip, I and the rest of my class teased Miss Kramer (now Mrs. Rix) mercilessly, threatening to arrive at school an hour late, as opposed to the unearthly hour of 6.45am which had been drummed into us for weeks. However, it turned out she had nothing to worry about, as everyone turned up on time and had everything they needed with them (even Years 8 and 9). Everything was going according to plan until it reached 7.45am and the coach had still not arrived.

"When the coach finally arrived and we were on the road, we realised we were running a bit behind schedule. However, it was not until we reached Dover that we realised we'd missed the ferry. But even that couldn't dampen our excitement. Our tour guide made sure we didn't get bored by regaling us with stories and information about every historic landmark we passed on the journey to Dover and even through France and into Belgium.

"However, our tour didn't end there. When we arrived at the first museum on our itinerary, the guide decided the sixth formers needed extra tuition on anything and everything to do with the First World War in the museum. When we arrived at the visual presentation, we presumed that the darkness was just a part of the 'blackout experience' but, unfortunately, this was soon followed by an announcement of 'technical difficulties', which we'd actually guessed from standing in the dark for five minutes.

"Following this, we partook in the trench experience, which gave us a small insight into the conditions faced by soldiers on the front line. I was shocked by how open the area around the trenches was and how shallow the trenches were in places, which is not something I had been expecting. I was moved by the experience and even more so by the sheer number of graves and names at the memorial sites we visited on the battlefields and the vast numbers of different nationalities of those who died on the battlefields in Ypres.

However, the most moving part of the day for me was the ceremony of the 'Last Post' at the Menin Gate. Seeing so many people commemorating those who gave their lives for their countries, and knowing that this ceremony takes place every day at the Menin Gate, was so moving that I know it is an experience I will not easily forget, and I'm glad about that. Of all the trips I'd been on at St. Bernard's, this was definitely my most memorable."

~~~~~~~~~~

Kim Fordham and her fellow Year 12 students outside the Cloth Hall Museum in Ypres, Belgium, in 2006

GEMMA GALBRAITH attended St. Bernard's from 2001 to 2008. She was elected head girl in 2007:

"Having just spent seven years at St. Bernard's, I can't think of anything at the moment even coming close to it. There is something about St. Bernard's that makes it what it is, a certain breed of teacher, and a certain type of student. If St. Bernard's were a credit card, it would definitely be a MasterCard; priceless.

BALLOONS ON APRIL FOOLS' DAY

"To most of the upper sixth, April Fools' Day is considered to be one of the most important days in the school calendar. After a few days of research, we decided that filling Miss Hayes' office with balloons sounded like a good plan. Our first challenge was to work out how many balloons we would need, which would involve a good deal of mathematical calculations. Whilst the occupant was away, I went and measured the length, width and height of the head of sixth form office in order to work out the volume. With this in hand, we now needed to know the volume of a standard balloon, and so discretely questioned Mr. Clancy about this.

"The final outcome was that we would need around 800 balloons. With the whole of the sixth form conscripted into service, it took us three days to fill enough balloons, with the added help of a handy helium canister. Storing the balloons was another challenge, as they had a tendency to spill all over the big and small common room, spectacularly blowing our cover. We had to fill over thirty black bin sacks, and hide the other balloons in various places around the common room.

"Finally, Thursday evening came. Cautiously waiting until after 4.30pm (when Miss Hayes had left), we began to carry sack after sack to the top of the brown wooden staircase, and empty them into the room. It took us until about 6.00pm and countless trips up the stairs, but the workout was worth it.

"We arrived back at school at 8.00am the next day (Friday) to await Miss Hayes, and hid in the small interview room next door. Upon hearing the unmistakable noise of heels on the wooden stairs, laughter almost overcame us, but we held it together and listened intently to the halt of the footsteps and the suspicious 'Oh, no …!' What a moment.

HIDING IN HISTORY

"This became a particularly enjoyable past time for me in my final year, as both Mrs. Ronan and Mrs. Rix's rooms are full of brilliant places to cram students into.

"St. Bernard's is generally full of brilliant places to hide, the attic was a favourite for our English class, the cupboard in E32 could fit a sizable number of people, but we also attempted lockers, bushes and roof tops.

"Friday, 7th December 2007 was a truly surreal day, which began quite innocuously with a charity fancy dress day. A group of friends and I all decided to go as forms of weather, and I was elected the role of 'cloud' (which later seemed to be a topic of great controversy as I was reported to be dressed as anything from a snowman, to a sheep). I had also been asked to read the 'examination of conscience' at the service of reconciliation that afternoon, which also proved to be an interesting experience as I looked out upon a congregation of fairies, smurfs, mermaids, and other fictional characters, asking them to examine their 'own appearance and not to judge that of others'.

"It also happened to be a close friend's eighteenth birthday that day and so, as is custom in the sixth form, we had a cake prepared for lunchtime.

"Now, whilst I can be sensible when called for, common sense seems to be an entirely different matter, and so it didn't really occur to me that a costume made from cotton wool and P.V.A. glue would not mix well with a match to light the candles on a birthday cake.

"I don't remember much of the event itself. It was not until I was packaged up in clingfilm by firemen that I realised that I was somewhat incapacitated for the day. I was in an intensive care unit for one week, of which I don't remember much, although the medical staff took great pleasure in filling me in on what I had missed.

"Apparently, in my state of morphine-induced delirium I spoke in a Southern American accent for about five days, insisted on singing Christmas carols very loudly and was adamant that there was a cow on the end of my bed, trying to eat my supper each night. Well, to look on the bright side of things, at least my parents won't have to worry about any hallucinogenic experimentation at university. Been there, done that.

"Yes, this was an awful accident, an awful time for my family, and, of course, it would have been better if it had never happened, but it did, and so what else can you do. Chin up, carry on. Not only a very British outlook, but a St. Bernard's attitude too. However, at St. Bernard's you have the whole community to pick you up and carry you on. I am quite certain that the swift recovery I made would not have been possible without the support and prayers that I received from school, churches and other people who wrote to wish me well.

"The Christian ethos of our school has always encouraged us to think of others before ourselves, and has taught me to always think about perspective. There will always be somebody worse off than you, always somebody with a harder life, a heavier burden to bear, and I think that it has been this that, together with my friends, family, teachers and the rest of the school, has made all the difference. I owe an awful lot to St. Bernard's, not just in terms of education, but of the friends made, the life experiences gained and the memories that I will always have."

~~~~~~~~~~~

The Head Student Team 2007-08, following their 'gunging' during rag week.
From L-R: Charlotte Le Corgne, Gemma Galbraith, Stephanie Bigley

KATRINA WAYLAND left St. Bernard's in 2008 to attend university. She also remembers the balloon incident:

"Year 13 was one of the best years of my life at St Bernard's. Since we weren't going to be around for April Fools' Day, Gemma Galbraith, our head girl at the time, and a few others decided to pull an early April Fools' Day prank with the entire sixth form helping out to blow up balloons. Led by Gemma, a number of students snuck around the school after hours, making sure Miss Hayes had gone, and stuffed her room to the brim with balloons.

"I will never forget the assembly she gave the following day, exclaiming both her surprise and confusion, as balloons seemingly 'avalanched' out of her room.

"Early January 2008, just after the Christmas holidays had finished, we had been told that only cold food would be available from the canteen. Curious, my class asked what was going on: 'People broke into the canteen over the holidays.' Although some of us were shocked, a lot of us couldn't help but laugh.

"We'd always believed that if someone broke into the school, it would be to steal computers and various other things, not to steal food."

~~~~~~~~~~~

MEGAN FANNING is currently in the sixth form at St. Bernard's. She explains:

"My school years at St. Bernard's were the best five years of my life. Every single student is given the greatest of opportunities; but it is up to us to grasp it with ambition, which I tried my best to do. One of the greatest experiences was the Year 9 and 10 production of *Oliver* in 2007. When the students heard about Mr. Clark's (the drama teacher) chosen play, there was a buzz of excitement in the air, but we never stopped to realise that most of us would have to play boys, seeing as it is an all-girls' school. That is how I landed my role as Fagin, which was enjoyable, and an amazing opportunity. With the inspiration of Mr. Clark, all the girls managed to become their characters, and the show was the greatest success. I was the last on stage, and I can still remember the outburst of cheers from the adrenaline-ridden girls as I sang my last line. We had experienced something amazing together as a group, which left us with feelings only we will ever be able to describe.

"School trips were seen as an occasion to see what teachers are like outside of school, and we certainly did on the history trip to Ironbridge in Shropshire 2007. Our two history teachers, Mrs. Ronan and Mrs. Rix, led us on a thrilling adventure to look at the first iron bridge. We were not too excited at the prospect of look- ing at different types of iron and locomotives, but we began to see the more human sides of the teachers.

"I had the privilege of walking through ankle-high mud in leather pumps with my history teacher Mrs. Rix, who also had not worn the most sensible of shoes. I mean, I had heard the memo about waterproof shoes, but wellingtons really did not match my outfit. It was an excellent chance to bond, pulling each other through mud, while the group in sensible shoes were already an hour in front of us. I think Mrs. Rix definitely saw another side to me. The history teachers were always a main source of entertainment, if not in mud, then on stage, dressed as Shirley Bassey, which I think Mrs. Ronan did brilliantly.

"Overall, my time was memorable, as I am sure many others have said, but it would not have been half as good without the wonderful teachers who support you through your five-year journey. You start in Year 7 as a child and, when you leave, they have moulded you into an adult with their knowledge and wisdom."

~~~~~~~~~~

EMILY RAY also remembers a memorable school trip to Poland and Berlin in 2007:

"The sixth-form trip to Krakow and Berlin is one trip that has really stood out during my time at St. Bernard's, despite each year being littered with various excursions. Open to students studying history, religious studies and German, the trip allowed us to visit the plethora of Poland and Germany's attractions. Auschwitz Concentration Camp near Krakow opened our eyes to the repercussions of Nazi Germany in a way that cannot be experienced through reading textbooks or watching videos. Retracing the steps of victims of the Holocaust, and witnessing the tactile remains of thousands of people, brought a much-needed sense of reality to our studies, in order to emphasise that history is far more than facts and figures; it's about emotions, too. The poignant hostility of the place is a feeling that lingered with me for some time.

"Although the trip had a serious tone to it, there were still many fun moments during the week, which allowed us possibly to drive the whole of the teaching staff accompanying us insane, the highlight of which was probably the nine-hour overnight coach journey from Poland to Berlin. Expecting a five-star luxury coach fitted with beds, we were less than impressed when a tiny bus pulled up outside our hotel. Having been told it was likely to be 'freezing' (in fact, it was sunny for pretty much the whole week), I was a little over-zealous with my packing, stashing a metallic cover in my bag, the kind which you would expect to use if trapped in your car surrounded by snow. After fifteen minutes under the cover, I emerged feeling like a roasted Christmas turkey. To make matters worse, when we did eventually arrive in Berlin, tired and grouchy, Mrs. Ronan treated us all to a 'gentle' two-hour walk around Berlin, a walk that resembled more of a marathon than a stroll. Mr. Cormican even fell asleep at the top of the Reichstag building. It was all made much better by the fact our hostel had an Internet café, which became the second home of most of us as we chatted to mates online and researched shops nearby that we fancied visiting. My friend Loriley and I researched vintage shops in Berlin for hours, and tried on several occasions to make a break for it, but we just weren't quick enough.

"Another major highlight was the trip to the KaDeWe, the largest department store in Europe. I doubt the staff knew what to expect when we were unleashed into a flurry of designer clothes and expensive food. We got a number of chances to shop during the week (little things please little minds …), although this usually resorted in a number of us rushing past the inspiring market stalls, selling traditional German and Polish goods, and straight into H&M and McDonald's. What a cultural bunch we were!

"Believe it or not, we did actually learn more from the trip than the price of the souvenirs converted into pounds and Euros. The Wieliczka Salt Mines (with a rather pleasant gift shop) and Krakow Cloth Market (again, with an enlightening set of stalls and merchandise) did provide an educating glimpse into another culture, whilst the array of museums and seminars we attended helped enrich our knowledge of Nazi Germany. If only every school trip was like this one."

~~~~~~~~~~

Anne Odeke attended the school from 1997 to 2004. She was head girl in her final year:

"Q. Who would ever have thought it possible to create a musical based on the Millennium Bug?

"The memories I have of St. Bernard's are some of the best memories I possess. Many of them involve laughing, driving teachers mad and going on school trips, but one of my fondest memories is of the school play 'Bytes: The Musical'. 'Bytes' was a musical that had been written by Mr. Clark (the drama teacher), Mrs. Maltby (the music teacher) and head girl at the time, Kate Lloyd.

"As we all know, all St. Bernard's girls are drama queens at heart and so, on the day of the auditions, there was a great buzz in the school. I remember auditioning for a number of parts, such as: Percy the P.C., Daisy Floppy Disc, The Hacker, etc. Therefore, you can imagine my surprise when I looked at the casting list and saw that I had been given the part of the evil 'Millennium Bug'. I was slightly confused and had a few questions on my mind ...

"Question 1: How does an actor get herself into the mindset of a computer virus?

"Question 2: What ghastly costume would Mr. Clark put me in? (neither my mum nor I at the time possessed the skills to create a worm outfit).

"Question 3: What sort of songs do computer viruses sing?

"Rehearsals began almost immediately. Play rehearsals were always fun and were a great opportunity to make new friends and hear the latest gossip, i.e. 'What do you mean Mr. and Mrs. Clancy are married? Who told you that?'.

"Unlike previous productions, we performed 'Bytes' at the New Empire Theatre, which I remember made me feel ever so professional.

"I was so proud when all my friends and family came to support me and was so chuffed that all of them had such a great evening. I remember at the time there was talk of there being a 'Bytes 2', but it never came about, so I challenge the current drama department to create something as original and, when they do, I hope they give me a ring as I'd certainly consider being in it.

"I wonder what part they'd have me playing this time?"

~~~~~~~~~~

THÉRÈSE SULLIVAN also attended St. Bernard's at the same time as Anne. She was deputy head girl in her final year, and has now returned to the school as an R.E. teacher.

"I have many fond memories of my time as a pupil at St. Bernard's. One that sticks out in my mind though is the Year 13 passion play that has become a tradition as part of the Easter Mass.

"Hours were spent organising people into groups – who would be in charge of costumes and props? Who would take control of the music? Who would write the script? I was one of those involved in the latter, which was an incredibly long process that I remember causing many disagreements. Some of us treated it as if it were a West End production and devoted hours to it. After all, who needed 'A' levels when we had this to put on our C.V.? Luckily we had a number of people in Year 13 at the time who were very creative (not being one of them, I got the part of chief priest 1, which has turned out to be my one and only ever acting role), so in the end it all came together beautifully.

"It is these traditions like the passion play, rag week and the pancake races that make St. Bernard's what it is – a place where everyone has the opportunity to get involved, in a good way usually – and why most never forget it in a hurry."

~~~~~~~~~~~

Nicola Reynolds remembers in particular an assignment she was given for media studies:

"Our media class made a video of Bill Bailey's *Insect Nation*, which naturally involved running around the school, filming ourselves doing strange things, most notably, myself jumping out of the bushes adjacent to the Bernadine Hall, dressed in a leather trench coat, a black beanie hat over my face, and sunglasses over the hat … to the very confused looks of Year 7 leaving their assembly, to then be greeted by Mrs. Hackett: 'What are you doing Nicola?'"

~~~~~~~~~~~

Leah Smith remembers her last day at St. Bernard's:

"I distinctly remember trying to get our whole year group to 'disappear' on our last day of school by hiding in the P.E. showers … everybody was crammed in and hushing everybody else. We constantly kept watch for teachers looking for us, and we screamed when we thought someone was close by, ready to catch us. In the end we were caught from all the noise we were making and everybody ran as fast as they could out of the two exits."

A Midsummer Night's Dream 2008; one of the magical productions now performed in the Bernardine Hall

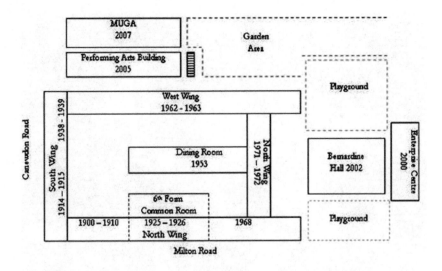

A plan showing the various extensions to the original building over many years

Chapter 11

The Nuns

Memories of the Bernardine Community

SISTER MARY LUCY (MAUREEN CLOWERY)
"I remember arriving at St. Bernard's in September 1943. I settled in very happily and was very upset to hear that a bomb had damaged the school in December 1943. When school reopened in January 1944, not all areas were ready for use. Being first years, we were 'on the move', going from class to class wherever a room was empty. A wonderful way to have a good excuse for being late.

"It was wartime, so if the air-raid siren sounded we all had to go to the dark damp shelter under what was the hockey field.

"I remember:

"White dresses and gloves for Reverend Mother's Feast Day and

for prize-giving.

"Miss Angel's spectacular nativity plays.

"Sister Mary Vincent chasing us out of the cloakroom on dull or cold days, her mission stall etc.

"Sister Mary Mildred's quiet but imposing authority.

"Many nuns and teachers – too many to list but all remembered.

"Little did I think when at school, that I would be back years later as Reverend Mother."

Sister Maria Whisstock

"I never thought that I would become a sister with the Bernardines, with whom I had been at school at St. Bernard's, but I did. God works in mysterious ways.

"There are so many memories I have of St. Bernard's that it is difficult to highlight them all. I was very much in the music scene, playing violin in the school orchestra, which had quite a talented string section in those days. There was the annual Christmas carol competition for the first to third years (Years 7-9) prepared in the music lesson, with the best group performing their work at the Christmas concert. I remember being part of the cast in *Oliver*. The junior choir performed in the local music festival in 1974-75. I'm not sure if we gained a prize, but our music teacher inspired us and there was no lack of students in the choir.

"Other memories include: the sisters and teachers who made a difference; the yearly educational visit; standing in height order (tallest at the back) in rows for assembly in the hall (now the library-resources area); playing in the school tennis tournaments and hearing of the sudden death of Pope John Paul I after only one month's pontificate. The news was relayed over the loudspeaker to each class by Rev. Mother, Sr. Mary Edmund.

"My class was what you might call today 'high maintenance' – lots of lively intelligent characters that I still meet with from time to time with lots to share and reminisce. I think most of us at least have become well-balanced, mature people, ready to give something of what we have received, in order to make our tiny but yet significant contribution of service in God's world. As Mother Teresa said, without our drop, the ocean will never be the same. So thank you St. Bernard's, and may you continue to inspire and educate in the love of God."

SISTER MICHELLE MARIE (TERRY THOMPSON)

"I was at school at St. Bernard's from 1957 to 1962. I was in Clairvaux, had a blue badge and enjoyed the spirit in the house. Speech days were wonderful events.

"I was in the choir of the famous nativity plays, and we had to learn thirty carols off by heart – no songsheets were allowed on the day. I was in one of the last years to have school dinners in the hall before the canteen was built. The first Friday masses were a novelty at first, but eventually there was a really good crowd there. After mass, Sr. Gabriel gave us a bowl of cornflakes, toast and a big cup of tea, all for three old pence.

"I was at St. Bernard's for the blessing of the 'new' building, which was then the sixth form area. Fr. McEvoy blessed it. A few days later he died while having his supper in the board room near the front door. I was the one who found him.

"I remember playing scrum with my friend Barbara Tearle and, when I entered the community, some past students called me the 'scrum sister'. I remember playing pirates in the gym at the end of term and, one day, I had a race up the ropes with the P.E. teacher, Miss Johnson. We finished neck and neck. I thought that was very sporty of Miss Johnson.

"One day, Sr. Mary Monica caught me with a bag of shrimps. I

had gone to the Convent for Mass and bought some shrimps on the way for breakfast.

"I remember Sr. Mary Vincent standing next to the tuck shop, collecting for the Bernardine School at Goma in [what is now] the Democratic Republic of Congo.

"I also appreciated the ice lollies that Sr. Mary Vincent made and sold in the summer, in aid of Goma."

Sr. Elizabeth Mary
(Elizabeth Mann)

"I belong to that unique generation of St. Bernard's students who can witness to both the 'before' and 'after' the nuns left. The Community announced its proposed departure during my third year (Year 9) and the Sisters left in the summer following my 'O' levels.

"I remember being fascinated by the school when I was young, since my mother had been a boarder there and had many a story to tell of her schooldays and the evacuation during the war to Rettendon and New Mills. It seemed to me that St. Bernard's would have nothing on those Enid Blyton tales of Malory Towers and St. Clare's.

"And my own memories ... well, on the first day, there was the obvious sense of relief that the school had moved on several decades. I remember the excitement of everything being new in those first few weeks: new friends, new teachers, new books, and of meeting up again with friends in older years. There was a real sense of having 'grown up' from primary school.

"I enjoyed both music and sports, making the most of any opportunity offered: orchestra, netball, table-tennis. Our class was lively and we never missed the opportunity of putting the board rubber just out of reach of a particularly short member of staff. I remember some excellent school trips, particularly the walking weeks to Hyning and the Lake District.

"There was also the joy of getting to the fifth year (Year 11), so that we could go into Southend at lunchtimes or down to Peter Pan's playground (not to mention swapping the blue-white checked blouses for a plain white one).

"Starting sixth form seemed another world: we had free lessons on our timetable (sorry, 'study times') and, for me, there was the relief of dropping all those subjects that involved the horrors of writing essays, in favour of my preferred maths and sciences.

"Although I was totally unconscious of it during my years at St. Bernard's, I guess that the Lord was working on me in secret. The Community's presence throughout those young teenage years served as a reminder of the spiritual dimension of life."

MEMOIRS BY **SISTER JOSEPHINE MARY** (JOSEPHINE MILLER)
"I was a pupil at St. Bernard's from 1959 to 1966, having previously been at 'Lindisfarne', the Preparatory School for St. Bernard's that has long since closed.

"When I think of my years at St. Bernard's, I remember the friendships – lively, argumentative, very enjoyable – a few of which lasted for many years.

"I remember some excellent teachers, notably in modern languages and Latin, who gave me such a good grounding, not just for further studies, but also for life in general.

"There was a lot of music, singing and drama, to a very high standard, and I joined in enthusiastically. The famous actress Helen Mirren was a memorable 'Eve' in the nativity play. These plays were performed annually for years, and were so much appreciated.

"I wasn't so good at sport, and hated hockey, but did a lot of ten-

nis, swimming and netball. Once, and once only, I was shooter for the fourth year netball team against Westcliff High, and we won.

"Religion was taken seriously, and lessons were full of discussions, but the teaching was solid.

"The sisters of the community were very present and obviously concerned for our welfare, human as well as spiritual.

"There were opportunities for good spiritual nourishment and growth, for those who wanted it, but this was never forced on us.

"Gradually, and with no pressure from anyone, I became aware that God was calling me to be a Bernardine. I answered that call, and have never regretted it, even if the path has not always been simple. God's call is always to life, growth and happiness, and so it has been for me."

SISTER MARY STEPHEN

"My first memory is of arriving for my first day at the school at the age of eleven, only to discover that I was wearing the wrong socks. Someone had told me you had to wear long socks and everyone else was in ankle socks. I remember feeling tearful. But in fact there were many more important things happening in the world at that time which, had I realised it, would have put all my worries about starting secondary school into perspective; the world was at war and had been so for nearly four years. This fact came home to me, perhaps for the first time, when, at the end of that first term, just before Christmas, a bomb dropped on some houses in St. Vincent Road, right opposite the school.

"I had gone to the Odeon cinema that evening with my mother and, although I cannot remember the film, I do remember the ter-

rible thump and all lights going out and a message coming up on the screen saying that a bomb had dropped somewhere behind the cinema. What struck me too was the awesome silence as everyone filed out of the cinema.

"When we arrived home, I learned exactly where the bomb had fallen and that the Convent, my wonderful new school that I had already begun to love, had been badly damaged. I was inconsolable. I remember, too, Fr. Whitfield at mass the following Sunday in the Sacred Heart church, saying that some of the nuns had been injured, and that started me off again. In fact, I think we were told later that only one sister had had a cut on her head, but they were all badly shocked and had been put up for the night in various places in Westcliff, including Nazareth House.

"I'm not sure what happened next or when we were allowed back into the school, but I do remember that, because my classroom was on the front of the house, which was the part badly damaged, I was not allowed to get my things and never saw again the lovely new leather pencil case that I had been given to start school. More heartbreak.

"So what else do I remember from my time as a pupil? I remember the kindness of the sisters, especially Sr. Mary Vincent, a kindness which I think I, subconsciously, wanted to emulate, a kindness which seemed all part of their consecration to God.

"I remember being a very enthusiastic rounders player. Too enthusiastic, because I took part in a match the day before the Latin 'O' level and got concussion, which did not please my Latin teacher, Sr. Mary Aelred, at all.

"When the air-raid siren used to go and we had to go down into the air-raid shelters, I was always disappointed if it was during the Latin lesson, because Sr. Mary Aelred insisted on continuing the lesson down there.

"While I was at the school, it was divided into camps and not houses. I suppose this was because of the names: Saxon, Roman, Briton and Norman.

"I was a Briton and had a red badge. If you were particularly badly behaved, you were 'decamped', and one of the results was that you had to sit at a desk right next to the teacher's desk.

"From that very position, I vividly remember trying to blow down the big Bible pictures that Sr. Marie Bernarde, a French sister, balanced on the blackboard ledge when she was teaching us R.E. I think we really loved this sister, but we did give her quite a hard time. Still, she was the sister who one day put the question to me: 'Do you really want to be mediocre all your life?' That made me think: No, I did not want that. And maybe that was the beginning of my journey in faith, which led me to become a Bernardine myself.

St. Bernard's gave me so much, humanly, intellectually and spiritually, as a child, a teacher and a sister. I remember my friends, my teachers and all the sisters with much love and gratitude."

Chapter 12

Head Teachers

Timeline of of Head Teachers

1910	Dame Lucie Destailleurs
1925	Madame Mildred
1962	Sister Mary Aelred
1966	Sister St. Michael Gibbons
1969	Miss E. O'Shaughnessy
1976	Sister Mary Stephen
1983	John Ballard
1995	Vicky Squirrell
2005	Pat Barron

Sister Mary Stephen

"I was the first, and the last, ex-pupil of St. Bernard's to become head teacher, there and, before I took up the post, it seemed an awesome task indeed. There were teachers on the staff who had known me as a child in the school, and I had not been a very easy pupil to cope with.

"That fact was brought home to me quite forcibly a short time after I began as head. A girl, whom I had been dealing with on a quite regular basis, was in my office for the 'nth' time, and I was trying to get her to see reason. She had obviously had enough, and suddenly she burst out: 'You can't talk! Apparently you weren't much better when you were at school – my mum's told me all about what you got up to!' However, I must say that those teachers who had had to put up with me in class were very supportive of me in my new role as head.

"Looking back on my time as head I mostly remember the warm and friendly atmosphere in the school, and I think it is true to say that it was rare for staff or pupils not to settle in there. One of the main challenges was trying to ensure that the different gifts of all the pupils were recognised and developed. Some were highly academic, some were gifted artists or musicians, some were budding sportswomen and others would find any excuse in the world in order to avoid having to go on to the sports field.

"The dual examination system, G.C.E. and C.S.E., helped to a certain extent, because a high proportion of the pupils did a mixture of both, and this meant some intermingling of classes. The system itself, however, was divisive and a nightmare for whoever compiled the timetable.

"The house system brought pupils together, as did the excellent plays and musicals. I remember, particularly, the production of *Oliver*, and cannot hear some of the songs without seeing the girls who sang them. I remember, too, with glee, being told that the then deputy headmaster, who was playing the role of Fagin and towards the end of the show had to strangle Nancy, whispered as he did so: 'I've been longing to do this!' She was a lovely singer, but apparently she had been playing him up a bit. We all, the girl included, had a good laugh about it.

"Other memories include the annual Christmas bazaar; the packed hall and me, standing on the stage with the microphone, trying to get my voice over the Christmas music that filled the hall, in order to encourage the buying and selling. All the time, Sr. Mary Vincent was happily raking in money on her piety stall for our community and school in Africa.

"Then there was the Junior Presentation Evening in July, when the first year classes recalled the past year, and you were never quite sure what was going to come out. I remember, too, the sports days 'up on the field' and the fund-raising fun days. I am sure there were hard times, too, but they have got lost amidst the warm, friendly times.

"My saddest moment was sitting in the staffroom next to the Reverend Mother General when she announced to an unsuspecting staff that the Community were leaving Westcliff. After a stunned silence, one teacher asked: 'And where is Sr. Mary Stephen going to live?' presuming that I would stay as head. 'She will be leaving with the community,' came the answer, and so I did. But I have never forgotten those happy times and, whenever I go back to the old school, it is always as if I am going home."

JOHN BALLARD

"It is a little daunting to attempt to summarise twenty-five years at St. Bernard's in the few words required for a contribution to this collection of memories. I could reel off details of incidents, such as when a visiting member of staff got herself locked in, after the school had closed for the night, and had to climb out through a window ... or name the elderly French nun, who would stop a girl from running in the corridor by neatly extending her walking stick in the girl's path. I have resisted this temptation, and instead, since I have a somewhat unique perspective on the years 1970 to 1995, have decided to restrict myself to those moments and events which, not only loom large in my memory, but will also resonate with all those who remember the 1970s, 80s, and the early 90s.

"My first visit to St. Bernard's was in 1968. I was teaching at Southend High School for Boys at the time. There had been great discussion in the staffroom about the proposal to make all secondary schools 'comprehensive'. The staff in grammar schools felt very threatened, as many had no experience of dealing with the broad range of students.

"Since I had previously worked at the South East London Comprehensive School for Boys, I was asked to attend local meetings relating to the implementation of the new Labour Government's plans to 'reorganise secondary education on comprehensive lines' [Hansard, January 1965].

"Change was very much in the air. The introduction of comprehensive schooling involved the raising of the school leaving age from fifteen to sixteen for all secondary school children. There had to be a new leaving examination, the recently introduced Certificate of Secondary Education.

"It was most significant that meetings of teachers to plan for these important developments in Southend were held at St. Bernard's where, because of the school's wide intake in terms of ability, a great deal of progress had already been made. So it was that I found myself sitting in Room 4, then the 'Junior Library', discussing how it was possible to teach French to children judged to be 'non-academic', and what the likely reactions of students would be, when they were told that they had to spend an extra year sitting at their desk before being allowed to leave school.

"I joined St. Bernard's in September 1970 as head of the modern languages department, which had built up a fine reputation and enjoyed high standards. I was well supported by six experienced members of staff; two members had been previous heads of the department (Mrs. Wade and Mrs. Greaves) and a third was the deputy head (Sister Mary Stephen). It was comforting but a little unnerving.

"Exam results were good, in both G.C.E. (sat by the two grammar forms) and C.S.E. (sat by the two modern forms). 'A' level French groups were second in size only to the English groups.

"The annual Modern Language Association Verse Speaking Competition attracted a large number of entrants, and St. Bernard's regularly featured among the winners. The French exchange was with a school in Calais. It was hard work finding students willing to go, as Calais did not seem all that different from Southend-on-Sea.

"A former French assistant and her husband (a teacher of English) lived in the Gers, a department in Gascony in the southwest of France, the home of the Three Musketeers.

"We decided to set up an exchange, flying French and English children to their hosts, at Easter and in the summer holidays. By chartering planes and filling them both ways, we were able to keep the costs down. Nineteen days in the foothills of the Pyrenees for £20!

"Other schools joined the scheme and, at one point, we were chartering Viscount aircraft which could seat 147. Thus 280 English and 280 French students benefited from the exchange that year. This was known as the 'Armagnac – East Anglia Exchange' and, I am sure, made a major contribution to French learning in the area. As a result, several good linguists went on to pursue their studies at the highest level, and firm friendships were established, which may even exist to this day.

"When I was appointed as deputy head at St. Bernard's in 1976, I was asked to stay on as head of modern languages (this was not unusual at St. Bernard's. Sister Mary Stephen had been both Head of R.E. as well as being deputy head – and still taught some French). A year or two later, I had to stop running the exchange, and responsibilities for this passed to another school. Such exchanges were so beneficial, linguistically, socially and culturally, but sadly they would be difficult to operate under the strict Health and Safety rules in place today.

"My seven years as deputy head, were very busy but happy ones. I was originally appointed as the sole deputy, but soon I was informed by the head teacher, Miss O'Shaughnessy, that the school now qualified for two deputy heads and that the governors were advertising for another deputy. Miss Fossey was appointed, and took over responsibility for the timetable and the curriculum, while I managed pastoral care and the daily deployment of staff.

"It became increasingly apparent to me that, as a community, the school was not being best served by the system of dividing 'selective' and 'non-selective' pupils into separate forms. I was well aware that the governors were keen to maintain the 'bilateral' nature of the school, so as to be able to compete with the local grammar schools, but having a system where a girl was labelled a 'grammar' or a 'modern' did little for social cohesion in the school. 'Grammars' could have an inflated view of their aptitudes and abilities, while 'moderns' could be resentful and live down to their perceived classification. The two streams rarely mixed. The house system did not really function. Naturally, some members of staff preferred to teach one stream rather than another. The whole system was divisive. I resolved that, if I had the opportunity, I would argue for change.

"Forms or 'tutor groups', containing girls of all academic abilities, were introduced shortly after I was appointed head. Subsequently, heads of year were appointed, and a fully integrated pastoral system was set up. This allowed for a meaningful house system to be created based on the tutor groups.

"There have been some magnificent theatrical and musical productions at St. Bernard's over the years, and it was no surprise that the school later acquired speciality status as an arts college.

"I am no great performer, and a reluctant one at that, but I was very proud to be associated with the musical *Oliver*, which was co-directed by Mrs. Stanworth, head of music, who was shortly due to leave St. Bernard's. *Oliver* was to be her last performance. She used this fact to persuade me to take part.

"There are three principal roles in *Oliver* that really need male actors and, in those days, there were no boys in the sixth form and only a few male staff. Mr. McEvoy was asked to play the beadle, Mr. Bumble. Mr. Hind was asked to play Mr. Brownlow, the kindly gentleman who took Oliver in.

"I was asked to play Bill Sikes, who murders Nancy on stage. Mrs. Stanworth said it was a good role for a deputy head, but I did not feel happy strangling one of my pupils. The production was a huge success because of the hard work of all those involved. There were some outstanding performances, in the roles of Nancy and Fagin, but Maria Wilde's Oliver was unforgettable.

"When the Bernardine Sisters announced their intention to withdraw from Westcliff, it was a cruel blow to the school. It is a common saying that St. Bernard's was more than a school; it was also a home. St. Bernard's was about to lose something so special that some feared it would change irrevocably. Change it did, but I hope and believe that the spirit of the Bernardines lives on.

"St. Bernard's Convent High School never closed while the nuns were in residence – except when they were all in chapel. The head's telephone number was the school number, day or night. There were nuns to chat to at break and lunch time. Sister Marie Hedwige and Sister Mary Vincent could be seen regularly in the cloakrooms keeping an eye on property and pupils. The nuns were also a force in the classroom – although that gradually diminished with the introduction of more lay staff. Also, the Sisters were praying constantly for all our needs.

"Their departure, in 1983, coincided with momentous upheavals in the education world. Prime Minister Callaghan had started the ball rolling in October 1976, when calling for a 'great debate' about the suitability of the education system to prepare young people for the modern world. This was to culminate in the Education Reform Act of 1988, which took the curriculum out of the teachers' hands and placed it squarely under the control of the Government. Up to then, the only subjects a school had, by law, to offer were R.E. and P.E.

"In the early 1970s, the birth rate had started to fall after the post-war 'baby boom'. By the mid-1980s, secondary school entries had begun to decline, causing fears of redundancy among teachers and severe staffing difficulties, as falling pupil rolls reduced the *per capita* income of schools. Also, by this time, teachers' salaries had ceased to match up with the level of responsibilities they were expected to shoulder. There was unrest in staff rooms across the land, as teachers reviewed the amount of voluntary, unpaid overtime they were prepared to put in at lunchtime, after school, in the evenings, at weekends and during the school holidays.

"These were unsettling times for St. Bernard's to open a new chapter in its history. However, with the support of parents, who continued to send their children to the school in good numbers, and with a loyal and hardworking staff, who kept St. Bernard's functioning even when many schools suffered strike action in February 1985, the school, on its small site at the junction of Milton Road and Canewdon Road, carried on and looked to the future.

"One tragedy marred the early years of St. Bernard's as it sought to establish itself under its new identity without the nuns – the death of Mrs. Oonagh Staddon. She was appointed deputy head to replace me when I became head. She had been teaching locally at Westborough High School, and had been waiting for an opportunity to join the staff at St. Bernard's. She was an immensely popular teacher and colleague. She was gentle, kind, capable and commanded respect. During the summer holidays of 1984, she was fatally injured in a car accident. This was not only a great loss to the school, but a huge personal tragedy to her friends and family.

"When they went, the Sisters left not only a void in all our hearts, but also empty rooms that had once been their living quarters. Those areas – formerly the nuns' cells, the scriptorium, needlework room, recreation room, 'Man of God's room' (for visiting clergy), kitchen, refectory etc. – had been strictly out of bounds to all lay members of the school.

"I well remember walking round them for the first time, and feeling very humble when I realised how simply, and in what restricted circumstances, the Sisters had lived in order to give as much space to the school as possible. They had literally moved up into the attic for us. This space was now available and had to be put to the best use possible. We decided that the chapel should be retained and made a focus within the school buildings.

"As the curriculum began to expand, so the need for more teaching space grew, and new classrooms were created on the top floor. There was no money for this straight away, but together with a willing caretaker, Mr. Charlie Carter, who fortunately lived practically on site next to St. Benedict's, the former Convent Guest House in Hermitage Road, we decorated and refurbished the areas ourselves during the holidays. St. Helen's Annexe had passed to the school by this time, and so the music and drama suites were formed.

"This was very much a period of rapid change. The older parts of the buildings were showing their age. The introduction of new subjects, like craft design and technology, and information technology needed more dedicated teaching areas. Temporary classrooms were set up by the Canewdon Road entrance.

"In addition, approaches to education were changing. Students were accorded more rights and respect. Learning was becoming more 'child centred'. Classrooms were being carpeted for the first time. Students could no longer store their books and belongings in their desks because desks were being replaced by tables, so lockers had to be provided.

"An example of how a change in the building brings about major change to life in school is the replacement of the old sash windows in the main building on Milton Road. Only senior students could be allowed to stay in, unsupervised, at lunchtime because of the danger of someone falling out of a window if the lower sash was raised. The new windows were safer, and girls did not have to pray for rain in order to spend a little time indoors.

"The night of 15th-16th October 1987 was one to remember. An unexpected storm had raged most of the night, uprooting trees, sending roof tiles crashing to the ground and interrupting electricity supplies to hundreds of thousands of homes in the south-east of England. There was an agreed procedure for closing schools when there was heavy snow, but this weather took us all by surprise. When I came into school, I discovered, among other damage, that the 'bike sheds' on the Canewdon Road side had been lifted by the force of the wind and blown over a two-metre high wall, to land in the middle of Canewdon Road. Those members of staff and pupils who had struggled in bravely were allowed to go home.

"In 1991, Local Management of Schools (L.M.S.) was introduced, giving governors and heads a greater say in how school funds were spent.

"In the case of St. Bernard's and most secondary schools in Southend, this was to lead to grant maintained status within a year or two. L.M.S. put an end to friendly cooperation between those schools and colleges, which hitherto had shared sixth form teaching of minority subjects like Latin and Japanese. Now we had to pay for our students to attend lessons at other institutions, and expected to be paid when others came to us. The publication of league tables increased competition between schools, but the Catholic schools, with their own special ethos, have survived and will, I am sure, continue to go on from strength to strength."

Vicky Squirrell

"When I joined St. Bernard's, I felt that it was almost predestined. I was born on St. Bernard's feast day, 20th August, and had been St. Bernard's house captain at school and now I was head of St. Bernard's School. I felt that it was a privilege to walk with the school for a period of time and I rapidly gained respect for the traditions and work of the community up to that time. I always knew I was standing on some memorable shoulders of the heads who had gone before me.

"In the nine years I travelled with the school, the scenery changed hourly, I remember long discussions about the pay-phone in reception and its possible misuse, but it was later replaced by probably 800 mobile phones; similarly, we always found outdoor space a problem, but two new large, buildings later ... In every aspect of our lives, the change was there and not just from within. One September, we came back having heard that Princess Diana had died, another September, the bombings in America – 9/11; – as a community we needed to learn rapidly and together how to cope. And we did!

"The constants were memorable too:

"Support from students, parents, friends of the school, staff and governors;

"The patterns of our daily life as a community;

"The masses, assemblies and spiritual life we shared;

"The friendships;

"Duke of Edinburgh Awards, skiing, activity holidays and trips;

"Charity work;

"Old Girls' events.

"All of these, and many more, for me form special memories, but for me one of the most important will always be how individuals brought their gifts and talents to our community, and cared."

Pat Barron

"In June 2004, I found myself sitting at one of the cafes under the Arches, dressed in my best black suit, carrying a laptop and looking out onto the estuary. The sun was shining. I had just been interviewed for the position of head teacher at St. Bernard's.

"I had only ever been to Southend on a couple of occasions before, having worked in Manchester and East London for most of my career. However, as soon as I arrived at reception, started a guided tour of the school and smelt the polish on the stairs, I was transported back to my convent school in Preston. I felt at home.

"When I joined the school in January 2005, the governors were close to completing a ten-year building programme, to provide an environment for learning that would meet the needs of the new century. The Performing Arts Centre was almost complete, with hundreds of boxes ready to unpack.

"The baton had been handed to me. I gave the school my commitment to keep all that was best of the school's traditions, and to make sure that the girls would be equipped academically, personally and spiritually to become confident individuals and responsible citizens.

"Developing young women and men as leaders has been a focus for us. All of our sixth formers now take on a formal leadership role, through the Community Sports Leaders Award, the Arts Council Arts Award, or the Duke of Edinburgh Award. Younger students take the responsibility of being members of the school council, liturgy prefects, and now, eco prefects.

"The students are proud of their school and are confident to 'have their say'. The school council worked with a landscape architect to redesign the Memorial Garden, which we all now enjoy. They introduced 'Fair Trade' and 'Justice and Peace' groups. This year they led the Languages Week. It has been a privilege and great fun to work with the five very different, but wonderful, head students: Zoe, Alice, Gemma, Melissa and now Hayley.

"The Arts have always been a central part of the life of the school. As an arts college, the school has been a spur for innovation and creativity; for reaching out into the community; for working with professional artists and for extending the curriculum to include: dance; music technology; theatre studies; three-dimensional art; graphics and the creative and media diploma. Dance and art have also brought a new dimension to our liturgies and to special events such as the Remembrance Service.

"Coming from a technology college, and years of teaching boys, for whom maths holds no fear, I felt it was important to create a culture of confidence in science and maths. Girls now study astronomy, robotics, statistics and mechanics. The number of girls who now choose to study maths and science at an advanced level is exciting. We were delighted to be asked by the Specialist Schools Trust to take on an extra specialism in science in 2008.

"At the turn of the twentieth century, the Catholic population in Southend was growing. The railway had brought families from London. At the beginning of this century, Southend is welcoming another group of new families; this time from further afield. St. Bernard's enjoys the variety of experiences brought to us by Catholic families from countries such as Poland, the Philippines, Latin America, Zimbabwe and China. They all receive the same warm St. Bernard's welcome that I did, and I hope they all feel 'at home'.

"As the head of St. Bernard's, I have found great support and strength in being part of a Catholic deanery. The head teachers and governors of all the deanery Catholic schools work together with families for the benefit of young people, from tiny tots to those going on to further education or starting work. St. Bernard's is not the only school celebrating an anniversary within the deanery this year. St. Thomas More School will have been established for 50 years in 2010, as will Our Lady of Lourdes Primary School.

"New technologies can be found throughout the school: video conferences, interactive whiteboards, and multi-media packages. Technology opens many opportunities for learning, but our students understand that it will never replace strong relationships based on trust and love. If young people are going to learn about, and accept, God's love, they have to experience it in every interaction they have with the adults around them.

In 2006, I asked Sister Mary Jo Martin to lead the whole staff in a day of reflection. Each of us renewed our commitment to the school's mission statement: 'love one another as I have loved you.' Each of us accepted a stone, painted with the word 'Communitas'. Visitors can see these on desks throughout the school. Each of us tries to live up to that mission statement every day. I would like to pay tribute to the staff, who give so much of their time and themselves to the young people in their care."

Judith Adams

Elizabeth Adams

Sara Adams

Helen Adey (Swettenham)

Kathleen Arvanitakis

Margaret Aston

Angela Atkinson

Susan Balkwell (Coles)

John Ballard

Eleanor Ballard

Alexandra Ballard

Georgia Bardua

Teresa Barker (Beechey)

Christina Barningham

Jane Barr (Denton)

Angela Barrett

Ursula Bartlett (Taylor)

Melinda Batchelor

Joan E Berry

Carmel Betsworth

Patricia Birch

Amy Bishop

Gerry Bishop-Laggett

Pat Blackford (Smith)

Amelia Blackstone Whines

Sharon Blainey

Liz Blair

Diane Bledsoe (Hudson)

Katie Blight

Pat Blight (O'Malley)

Carol Bohanna (Bromley)

Christine Boyden

Margaret Bradbury (Chaffey)

Marie Bradley (Webber)

Claire Bragg

Joan Bramley (Russell)

Patricia Brennan

Rosemary Brett-Pitt (Cook)

Clare Briscoe

Marie François Britt (Hurst)

Gary Broad

Katherine Brook

Elizabeth Brown (Connelly)

Marina Bryant

Alexandra Bull

Anneke M Bull (Lees)

Sarah Burns

Jean Burrow (Sibley)

Deborah Burrows

Joan Butcher (Carthew)

Anne-Marie Byrne

Roger Calton

Ruth Calver (Hannah)

Betty Campbell

Andrew Campbell

Mary Carey

Daphne R Carr

Susan Carter

Tony Castle

Victoria Catmull

Mary Chapman

Evelyn Charles

Patricia J Charlton

Anna Charters (Pearson)

Sheila Chesterman

Carol Choppen

Freda Choppen (Morten)

Karen Clancy

Vivienne Clancy

Mary Clark

Patricia Clark

Loulou Clark

Carol Clemesha

Melanie Codarin-White

Maureen Coghlan

Eveline Coleman

Wendy Collin (Mays)

Pierina Collini

Jeanette Collins (Latta)

Irene Conley

Mary Connelly

Pamela Cook

Mary E Cooper

Mary Cooper

Katherine Costello

Christine Cox

Margaret Cox (Pearcey)

Shiela Cray

Teresa Critcher

Clare Crossman (Duncan)

Louise Curtis (Felstead)

Sarah Curtis (Gentle)

Brenda Curtois
Kath & Julie Cushion
Caroline Cutts
Marjorie Dale
Julie Davidson
Kathleen Davies
Mrs Valerie Davies (Hockley)
Sally Dawes (Gravestock)
Jackie Dawson
Fiona Dedman (Fitzpatrick)
Ann Dick
Sharon Dierks
Hannah Dignum
Rosemary Dillon
Ann Dixon (Flaxman '49)
Stella Dobson (Parisio)
Ann Driscoll
Peggy Duckworth
Tessa Duggan (O'Leary)
Valerie Edmunds (Pinto)
Pat Edwards (Coles)
Maureen Egan
Michael Elmes
Sonia Ensom (Sherrard)
Rosemary Erricker (Coggins)
Nightingale Family
Shelton Family
Valerie Fane
Jean Fernbank
Mrs Elizabeth M Field
Margaret Fisher
Miss E Fitzgerald
Anne Flanagan
Fiona Flett
Kimberley Fordham
Annette Forkin (Richardson)
Angela Forrai (Lucking)
Marie Forsyth
Beryl Fox (Claydon)
Mr J & Mrs R Franklin
Michelina Freda
Rita French (Harcourt)
Judith French (Ross)
Karen Froydenlund
Linda Gaff
Gemma Galbraith

Sheila Gallagher
Margaret Gammon
Eve & Martin Garwood
Jennifer George (Morgan)
Joanna Geraghty
Peter Glassock
Susan Glassock (Sothcott)
Sophie-Rose Daubney Glover
Sheelagh Bernadette D Glover (Daubney)
Anne Godfrey (Baker)
Jessica Goldsmith
Judith Goodenough
Lesley Googe (Reed)
Anne Gornall
Tina Gould (Dickinson)
Peter Green
Audrey E Green (Restorick)
Marcia Gresham
Mrs B Gretton (Sutton)
Carol Griffiths
Karen Grimmett
Elisa Hall (Wall)
Catherine Hallam (Ballard)
Glynis Halling (Edwards)
Lynne Hamilton
Katherine Harms (Gravestock)
Margaret Harvey (Austen)
Jill Healey (Raymond)
Louise Hebden
Janet Hewitt (Towler)
Joanne Higgs
Mary Hillier
Alison Elizabeth Hillier
Dominique Hillson
Ann Hilton
Jessie Hodgson
Joan Hogg (Head)
John & Theresa Honeyands
Christine Horden (Simms)
Vanda Horton
Myrna Hubbard (Hurley)
Lauren Hudson
Mrs B Huggins
Pauline S Huntington
Mrs Joan Hurley
Jacqueline James

Jennifer Jenson
Una Johnson (Tamsett)
Nancy Johnston
Pauline Jordan
June Keast (Fowler)
Christine Keenan (Beechey)
Linda Kenton (Rothman)
Susan King (Poole)
Doreen Kirby (Bowles)
Dennis Knight
Fran Kramer
Hilda Kramer
Christine Lambert (Smith)
Anne Le Goff-Wilson
Gill Leadbetter (Stuchberry)
Sarah-Jane Lee
Sarah Lee
Mr David Lench
Margaret Lench
Joan Lench
Ann Lench
Pat Lewis
Jeanine Lewis
Claire Littley
Jackie Lovett (Edwards)
Eileen Jessie Lowe
Patricia Lucking (Denmead)
Mona Lynam
Pauline Lynam
Kathleen Lynam
Marie Lynch
Denise MacDermott (McCarthy)
Fiona Maltby (Ingham)
Shirley Malton (Soper)
Veronica Manly
Josephine Manning
Jane Martin
Caroline Mason
Patricia Mason (Fowler)
Barbara Mather (Cox)
Joan Maughan
Geraldine May
Rachel McCarthy
Elizabeth McConalogue
Mrs Wendy McCormick (Main)
Francesca McEvoy

Louise McGonagle
Barbara McHugo
Maureen McIver (O'Leary)
Lucy Merrett
Clare Mersey
Alexandra Mersey
Sr Josephine Mary (Miller)
Julie Milner (Pearson)
Andrèe Minois (Cole)
Lisa Morgan
Angela Morris (Gretton)
Carola Morton
Michelle Morton
Wendy Murphy (Harvey)
Bridget Mary Murray
Roberta Nichols (Coleman)
Angela M Niel (Little)
Denise O'Callaghan
Gill Oliver (Barr)
Una O'Reilly-Foley
Jo Orsi
Ann Overment (Rope)
Holly Owen
Sue Owen
Jean Sybil Pacey
Nicola Pain
Petra Parker
Fiona Partridge (Lucking)
Jacqueline Paterson (Lawton)
Felicity Pawsey (Ramsden)
Laura Peretti
Rachel Perkins
Frances Persighetti
Cassandra Pestana
Linda Petchey (Fowler)
Suzanne Phillips (D'Eath)
Sr Maureen Pike O.D.C
Christine Pinder
Marie-Thérèse Pinto
Anita Pirali
Marguerite Pirali
Susan Plastow
Christine Polson
Rita Poole (Pickrell)
Joan Popham
Judy Povey (Songhurst)

Brenda Powell (Vicary)
Ena Power (Vine)
Lauren Price
Kim Radford
Jane Rafter
Margaret A Raviens-Smith (Reader)
Laura Ravinet
Samantha Rawlinson
Jean Raymond (Twydell)
Sue Reynolds (Waddingham)
Katy Robertson
Rebecca Robinson
Christine Rolph
Bridie Ronan
Jennie Ronan
Chloe Rouse
Jayme Rouse
Louise Ruston
Jessica Ruston
Margaret Sanders (Saunders)
Ellen Saxton
Ethel Saywood
Janet Sherriff (Coggins)
Pauline Shorey (Edwards)
Gaynor Slattery (Smith)
Heather Smith
Theresa Smith
Maisy Smith
Grace Smith
Jean Smith (Baker)
Anne Smith (Price)
Carol Snelling (Guiver)
Mary Speakman (O'Brien)
Kathleen Spindler
St Peter's RC Church Eastwood
Catherine Stark
Tina Starmore
Patricia Stoat
Hayley Stockwell
Margaret Storey
Diane Marie Sullivan
Christine Sumpter
Mary Sutcliffe (MacHattie)
Caroline Swain (Lees)
Shirley B Swan

Fiona Swerdlow (Sim)
Molly Symmons (Pickrell)
Gillian Tattersfield (Mansfield)
Jennifer Thompson
Sandra Thompson
Sarah Thompson
Melissa Thomson
Megan Thomson
Jean Thornton (Pedley)
Julia Tideswell (Cox)
Alessia Tidman
Amanda Tisi (Tamsett)
Jean Tonking
Margaret Tothill
Mr A M Townsend
Sue Tye (Rope)
Nuala Wade
Valerie Walker
Mary Walpole (Hodder)
Natasha Walton
Yvonne Warren
Maureen Warren (Fitzpatrick)
Rosemary Weeks
Mrs A Welding
Karen Wells
Jenny Wheeler
Theresa Whitaker (Burry)
Monica White
Miss F White
Laura Whittle
Pamela Wilderspin
Gay Wilkins (Smurthwaite)
Daphne Wilkinson
Eileen Wilson
Amy Wilson
Anne R Wonnacott
Frances Wood
Shannon Wood
Sheelagh Woodfield
Constance M Woodman (Westwood)
Audrey F B Wright
Valerie Wroe
Johanna Wylde
Juliette Young